well
DESIGNED
life

well DESIGNED life

10 lessons in BRAIN SCIENCE & DESIGN THINKING for a Mindful, Healthy, & Purposeful Life

KYRA BOBINET, MD MPH

engagedIN

PRESS

If you are interested in bonus offers and other products on combining brain science and design thinking, or to inquire about keynote speaking or appearances, go to www.drkyrabobinet.com

Published in the United States by engagedIN Press,
offices in Walnut Creek, California.

www.engagedin.com

This book is not intended to take the place of medical advice from a trained medical professional. Readers are advised to consult a physician or other qualified health professional regarding treatment of their medical problems. Neither the publisher nor the author takes any responsibility for any possible consequences from any treatment, action, or application of medicine, herb, process, or preparation to any person reading or following the information in this book.

Book design by Katie Benezra
Editing and Neuroscience consultation by Stephanie Shorter, PhD
Copyediting by Ruth Strother

ISBN 978-0-9967345-7-8 (print)
ISBN 978-0-9967345-0-9 (ebook)

PRINTED IN THE UNITED STATES OF AMERICA

For my husband, Josh Leichter,

My kids,
Shara, Memphis, Ethan, & Alecsa

And in loving memory of
Irene Shuster

Contents

Preface

Why can't people change when they say they want to? And how can they?

I believe that unhappiness and suffering stems from not being able to change ourselves or our lives for the better. We may get stuck in grieving the loss of a relationship. We may feel stuck in a dead-end career. We may get injured or disabled and struggle to adjust. We may be a compulsive eater and out of control. Or we may have not achieved the peak performance we know is within us.

At one point or another, every person I know has been pinned down by life—unable to wriggle free for a time. Developing the ability to affect what, when, and how we want to change is a universal struggle. Regardless of our worldly success, we all share the very human experience of trying to change our behaviors only to sometimes fail, relapse, or get lost.

But there is a way out.

I am writing this book because I have tried to help people change. I have done this as a physician, volunteer, corporate executive, product/intervention designer, public health professional, nonprofit founder, faculty instructor, mentor, friend, mother, and wife. Sometimes I've succeeded; other times I've failed. This includes when I was working on myself. And after decades of iteratively changing my own life, as well as playing those many roles as change maker and innovator, I have discovered a universally reliable solution that draws on the rigors of science and the creativity of the human spirit. This book is about sharing what I have found so that others may benefit.

Notice that I said *iteratively*? Making real change in your life requires repeating something over and over, iterating, to make small changes each time. In Silicon Valley where I teach, iteration is a creative practice of design. Designers iterate on many versions of a product, tweaking to improve it and make it more successful. Likewise, I am proposing that we can change and improve any part of our lives through constant, unrelenting iteration. *Iteration* in this case means that we try and try and tweak and tweak the design of our behavior changes until we transcend.

There are two main points to this book. First, you are the designer of your life and your behavior change. Second, designers iterate their way to success—and that is how you will also succeed.

You may be surprised that I just called you a designer—it may not be a familiar term to you or maybe you have never thought of yourself as one. In my eyes, every human is by default a designer of their life because we all have one thing in common: choice. We choose our relationships, we choose our responses, and we choose how we solve problems. And what else is design but making choices consciously? You are in the role of a designer any time you shop for groceries, help a friend, make an appointment, or clean your house. In each case, your actions are communicating to the universe who you are, what you want to experience, and how you want to live. You design all of this—whether consciously or unconsciously.

The level of consciousness with which you do these actions is another matter. As the designer of your life, you may not act like it sometimes, maybe even often-times. Instead, you may give away your power or play a victim to life—we have all been there—until you figure out how to stop. That is where I believe thinking like a designer brings empowerment.

The mindset of a designer is one of actively creating and problem-solving—iterating their way out of sticky situations. In this book, I hope to prove to you that you are already doing this and to give you the tools to do it more often, with more awareness and skillfulness, and with greater results. I want to make it so that you can choose not to ever be a victim to anything or anyone anymore.

Years ago when I used to see patients, I noticed that there were two types of people—those who were actively controlling and iterating on their health and those who were not. This was my first hint that there is a solution for those who were not taking the reins—could it be better for them if they were more like those who were taking control? In fact, the last patient I remember treating was a 57-year-old gentleman who came in with a gouty toe. He shared with me that he took methamphetamine three days prior (which made him dehydrated, which in turn gave him gout). As I wrote the prescription for his gout, something turned inside me—this was not the conversation I wanted to have with people. I was far more interested in the behavior underlying his meth use. I wanted to go to the source of why he was not in control of his life and health.

So, I pivoted. I withdrew from pursuing residency and instead went to Harvard to study public health, behavior change, decision science, and population health. From there, I became a corporate executive, creating large-scale behavior change programs and products for millions of people. Then in 2013, the brilliant Dr. BJ Fogg invited me to Stanford to study in his lab and opened a whole new world to me—behavior design, a field he pioneered. From there, I started a design firm, engagedIN, as a practice that translates behavior and neuroscience into helping people to be the designers of their health, relationships, and lives.

This book marks a 20-year journey. I have been a geeky neuroscience hobbyist for decades—voraciously reading every new study that could offer insight into why we do what we do. With my insatiable curiosity, as well as my own 16 years of practicing meditation, I have compiled a number of reliable patterns that I believe define human behavior. In particular, I have found that how our brain operates determines whether we change our behaviors or not.

In just the past 10 years, researchers have discovered unprecedented insights into human behavior and brain patterns. This confluence of knowledge has offered a new opportunity to change our behaviors based on what we now know to be our irrational, impulsive, distractible, emotional, and complex brain.

I have picked my 10 favorite brain science concepts to share in the 10 chapters of this book because I want you to know what is really going on with you—what your brain is doing while you go about changing your life. I want you to be able to use hard, cold science—not just whimsical theories or inspirational quips from some author—as the basis for becoming a better designer of your life and your behavior.

To that point, I have simplified these brain science concepts for ease of use. In many cases, this reduces the science down to a metaphorical level because what I care about is that they can be applied easily toward design. As a former bench scientist and primary researcher, I respect the trade off between true neuroscience and applied neuroscience design as presented in this book. And while I may pick specific brain regions that are known for a certain function, like emotion, as a scientist I personally favor the emerging point of view that these functions are conducted across integrated, multi-focal regions of the brain.

Designing behavior is equal parts art and science. Steve Jobs once said, "Design is not just what it looks like or feels like. Design is how it works." Adopting the mindset of a designer puts you in the driver's seat of making life work. Grounding yourself in the science of how we see the world and how our brain responds helps you design behaviors that work—in real life, for real people. This is 100 percent about you acting on what you always wished you would do. It's about stepping out of any areas of helplessness and into creative self-direction. You have a choice: design your life or let it design you!

I want to acknowledge a few key mentors along my path, as I did not get here alone. First is the Great Spirit. Whatever or whomever that is to you, I fully acknowledge a mysterious, compassionate intelligence that has awakened me to serve the deeper patterns of life and behavior and be a codesigner with this Spirit. Second are my teachers: my daughters Shara and Alecsa; all the incarcerated youth I've worked with; all of my past patients; and mentoring and wisdom from Sylvia Gretchen, Josh Leichter, Curtis Wright, David Lewis, Dr. BJ Fogg, Sister Dang Nghiem, Dr. Shoshana Helman, Nghia Tran, Jon Young, Dr. Art Giacalone, and Paul Rafael. I want to express my deepest respect for the wisdom held across many world traditions and contemplative teachers, who offer stores of how to live well. Third, my collaborators: our extremely talented team of designers at engagedIN, Dr. Larry Chu (my brother from another mother) and the amazing e-patients of Stanford Medicine X, who stand for person-centered design and care; Dr. Jim Doty, who is spreading compassion throughout healthcare and beyond; Dr. Joe Kvedar, who is forging connections of care; Dr. Danny Sands; e-patient Dave; the Society for Participatory Medicine, which empowers people to take charge of their care; and the Mind Body Awareness Project, which is innovating at the intersection of social justice and inner empowerment through mindfulness. Finally, I want to thank the many researchers and scientists and designers whose work has taken our understanding of behavior to new levels—all of us are so fortunate to be able to make use of their insights and breakthroughs toward making this life more beautiful and meaningful for all.

①

design the change you want to see in your life

Design is simply to move from an existing condition to a more preferred one.

—Milton Glaser

S ara looked in the mirror and frowned. Where she wanted to see smooth areas of thigh and tush, the mirror was giving her something else altogether. She had a party to go to, she had a pair of gorgeous pants that she had splurged on, and she had the mirror, which was beginning to annoy her. She found herself thinking about how wearing control-top pantyhose under her dresses gave her the lovely smoothness that she really wanted here. But there was no way in hell pantyhose would work with this outfit. She refused to give up on wearing the pants, however, and soon found a pair of scissors in one hand and a pair of control-top pantyhose in the other. She cut the feet off of the stocking legs and tried them on under the pants. She glanced over her shoulder at the mirror and found that it now showed the image she had in mind.

Sara Blakely had just invented Spanx, for which we are forever grateful.

Many people are already familiar with Sara Blakely's story.[1] But the key part of that tale is the part most of us miss. Why did this young woman—who had been selling fax machines door-to-door for seven years—have the mindset that allowed her to come up with such a simple yet unusual life hack for herself? (Because solving a fashion challenge by chopping up one product to create a new one is solidly in the realm of the scrappy, do-it-yourself design!) And what was it that made her keep working to improve her newly invented body smoother garment, trying out one version after another until she found something that was useful to so many women?

Spanx is the creation of a woman who applied design concepts to solve an everyday problem. Sara wanted something different, so she experimented with that first crude prototype, then she made changes and tested versions until she got it right.

Sara had an advantage that most people never experience—she was raised by a father who pushed his children to think differently and embrace challenges and failure as a natural part of life. At the dinner table he would ask his kids what they had tried and failed at that day, and he would praise them for their attempts. The fundamentals of design were key to his philosophy (though he had probably never heard the term), and he shared that gift with his daughter, who ran with it.[2]

There's good news for all the rest of us not raised by Sara's dad, though. We can easily learn how to design elements of our own lives. We are used to designing outfits, room décor, and more and more things like holiday cards and Pinterest boards. But what about using the same design thinking to improve our health, our relationships, or our career? We are living in an era in which design is being applied in new and different arenas. Popular culture is full of examples, such as Pinterest, Instagram, Etsy, and the Maker Movement, demonstrating that there is a fundamental awakening of everyday people engaging in the design of their lives. In his 2014

New York Times article "A Golden Age of Design"[3] Rob Walker describes this momentum as "an unprecedented belief in the power of design to not only elevate an idea, but be the idea."

EVERYDAY LIFE, EVERYDAY DESIGN

A couple years ago, I found myself thinking often about how I might short-circuit my family's ever-increasing junk food habit and the extra fat and flab that went along with it. Something needed to change—for my kids' sake and for my own.

Soon after, I attended a team meeting in the lab of Dr. BJ Fogg. Dr. Fogg is the father of behavior design and the director of the Persuasive Tech Lab at Stanford University. He is also one of my mentors.

That day, Dr. Fogg set down a few clear glass containers in front of us. They were full of bright red strawberries and snap peas, and he told us to dig in. The food was from his garden, and it was delicious. I pounced on a particularly gorgeous strawberry. Fogg described working on a fridge design experiment in which he simply changed the way food was stored and arranged in his refrigerator. He put fresh, healthy food at eye level, hid the bad stuff in less visible spots, and used clear glass containers for storage, providing an unobstructed view of the healthy items that were available. With a few simple design changes, his family was eating healthier and cutting down on junk. I heard this and immediately thought of my girls. My mind had gone into high gear, plotting and planning. If Dr. Fogg's fridge experiment had worked for his own household, then hell yes, I was going to try it in mine.

When I got home that night, I reviewed the fridge, the pantry, and the facts.

Over the last couple years, my teenage daughters had gradually slipped into the habit of eating more and more junk food instead of the healthy snacks I had packed for them in grade school. Each day they scarfed down things like pretzels, cookies, and mini corn dogs, while the organic carrots and apples rotted like mold experiments in the produce drawer. My kids had started to gain some belly fat. I wasn't doing much better. As a woman over 40, and with an insatiable appetite to go with it, I grew a layer of fat on my back (aka my back blubber) that I hated with a deep ferocity. I desperately wanted my kids to develop healthy eating patterns that would support them in adulthood, but I could not figure out how to say something without harming their self-esteem.

I keenly remembered what it was like to be a teenaged girl—one raised on lots of fast food while growing up in Oklahoma— and the body image issues that came with it.

In came my first family food design. I decided to start small, so phase 1 of my design addressed just one behavior—my family's deep, abiding love of cookies. I threw out (and stopped buying) the junky chocolate chip variety that we'd been scarfing down and replaced them with a container of mini oatmeal raisin cookies made from simple, healthy ingredients. I then put the container in the freezer, which meant that it would have to thaw for a bit before we could comfortably chew the cookies. I also made sure that the cookie container stayed in the very bottom of the freezer, away from the top drawer where the healthy frozen meals and snacks were placed.

The geeky scientist in me was satisfied with Version 1. The mom part of me thought, *please let this work*. The behavior designer in me was ready to iterate.

A few weeks later, I realized that our cookie consumption had dropped significantly, and I did a little happy dance right there in the kitchen.

My small cookie experiment worked so well (and so quickly) that I arranged the rest of our fridge with the same principles in mind. I put fresh, healthy food at eye level and used only clear containers for storing these snacks, which provided an unobstructed view of the good choices. The containers and the overall presentation of the healthy snacks infused them with an attractive power—their bright colors caught your eye as soon as you opened the fridge. Those super healthy (and previously boring) fruits and veggies were now either the first to be grabbed or nothing was chosen and the fridge door was closed. Once the top-choice snacks were in place, I made sure that the less healthful ones were hard to reach or time-consuming to make. (Remember that one: I designed it so that the kids' laziness worked to their advantage!)

I wanted to be sure that my new food design went well beyond main shelves in the fridge, so the foods in the pantry and cupboards got the same treatment, and I made sure to place additional healthy snack choices out in the open for easy discovery. Good foods now ruled the roost and the junk food left the premises on trash day.

In the months that followed, I quietly watched my girls' eating habits (and mine) adjust to the new food design. My daughters snacked less, and when they did look for something to nibble on, they ate apple-sauce, high-fiber bars, and unbuttered popcorn—all prominently displayed in the snack drawers and on the shelves I had designed for them. Shocking behavior for teenagers, right? I'm happy to report that their belly fat faded away and my back fat shrank.

Just as I was able to be the "designer" of improving my family's nutrition, you can be the designer of your own life—any part of it or all of it.

DESIGN OR BE DESIGNED

Of course, other people—your spouse, partner, children, coworkers, parents, and friends—have influence, but in the end, what you can control in your life goes into only one of two buckets: what you choose to design and what you don't. Even if you have been sitting back passively and letting life happen to you, I want you to know that you have the power to use design to improve your health, your relationships, and your happiness—virtually every aspect of your life.

Before you protest, let me make one thing clear. Of course, you don't have control over everything that happens in your life or the world around you. Nobody does. People get sick, they get laid off, or they lose everything in a natural disaster. I get that. I truly do. I have been a single mother for 13 years and at one point, after years of running a nonprofit, I had just $4,000 and an old Subaru to my name. But I designed my way out of it and went back to graduate school at the tender age of 37.

After decades of changing human behavior—others and my own—I am thoroughly convinced that design skills are the single most important ability that we humans possess. It is our modern day equivalent to hunter-gatherer survival tools.

But, sadly, many people never tap into the vast amount of power they have to design the aspects of their lives that they *can* control. They drift along, leaving things to chance, and then wonder why life never seems to turn out well. And when things inevitably do go wrong, they drop their heads in defeat, accepting their misfortune, telling themselves there's nothing to be done about it.

Why is that? Why do we fail to break free of a bad situation, not grabbing the steering wheel of our own lives?

The number one reason we don't break free is simple. We stop trying. Why? Because we lose hope. And why do we lose hope? Usually, it's because we are playing a win-lose version of the game. We let our first attempts (aka our first design) count as wins or losses, instead of tweaking them or tossing them out and starting over with new ones. We accept defeat early on and we just stop trying.

Imagine if all the world's great inventions were abandoned as failures in their first version. Seriously, just think about that. Edison and Latimer would never have produced a lightbulb[4] that actually worked. Florence Parpart would not have graced us with the gift of the electric refrigerator,[5] and Alexander Graham Bell would have given up long before the telephone could make a call. Jobs' and Wozniak's Apple Computer would not have made it beyond a messy heap of parts in a garage. And if actress Hedy Lamarr hadn't been so bored by the bland roles that 1930s Hollywood threw her way, she would never have started inventing technologies that saved countless lives in World War II, technologies that make all wireless communications possible today.[6] These products were all designed, which means they went through tens, even hundreds, of failed versions (called prototypes) in order to eventually work. So, why do we think we must get it right in one try, and then when things inevitably go awry, why do we give up forever?

Elephants in captivity provide a perfect example of this behavior pattern. Maybe you've noticed that these massive creatures that weigh several tons can be held in place by just an ankle chain and a small stake, which is driven only a foot or two into the ground? They could easily use their incredible strength to free themselves, but they don't. That's because they were tied to that stake when they were small. Young elephants try to pull the stake from the ground, but they're not strong enough yet, so after a while they give up. By the time they reach adulthood, they've gotten used to their situation and don't realize that they now have the power to pull the stake from the ground with very little effort.

Think about that. Captive elephants spend most of their lives ignoring their immense power. And the same is true for many people. Like a baby elephant, we may try at first, but when things don't work out, we may settle for less. We unknowingly agree to live tethered to a stake that minimizes who we truly are, unaware that we have the power to break free.

Think back to a time in your life when you gave up on something. More than likely, you had set a goal and developed a rigid definition of what the eventual out-come would be. We've all been told that we should set goals and focus hard on them, painting a clear mental picture of what our lives will be like when we achieve them. We've imagined what we'll look like in a swimsuit after we lose 30 pounds, or picked out the car we'll buy when we get that new job, or set our sights on the beach house we'll get when we sell our first novel. That technique can be motivating, certainly, but it also forces you to take a pretty big gamble. The weight comes off but then we gain it back again. The coveted job goes to someone else. The book doesn't sell. Suddenly, your reality doesn't match the picture you had in your head, but since you believed in your exact goal so strongly, you no longer trust yourself. And rather than coming up with a new goal, or making it more flexible, you just give up. Sound familiar? There's actually a scientific explanation for this.

Researchers have found a small but powerful part of our brain that seems to keep track of our failures—the habenula. The habenula is not there to do harm; it actually is there to protect us. In theory, the habenula helps us learn what doesn't work so we can avoid wasting our time repeating the failed behavior again and again. This may well have inspired the saying "Once bitten, twice shy."

But the habenula works against us when we set a specific goal and define it in terms of winning or losing. Then if we don't achieve it, one of the things the habenula does is count it as a failure. It is thought that the habenula then suppresses our motivation to repeat that particular pursuit. At that point, we go into baby elephant mode. Even though we learned something valuable from our failed experiment, we think the stake in the ground is too strong, and our negative self-talk begins: "Been there, done that, got the T-shirt," "Well, that sure didn't work," or "I can't do it, so why bother?" We did not reach our stated goal, so we gave up.

If you've tried to lose weight or stop smoking without conscious behavior design, chances are good that you were not successful. Maybe you intended to get up early and go for a run, but instead you hit the snooze button. The habenula notices and starts keeping score—you're 0 for 1. Your goal is to gradually cut down on cigarettes, but at the end of the day you've smoked as many as you usually do. Now you're 0 for 2. You promise yourself that you'll cook a healthy dinner tonight—with vegetables this time!—but the pizza delivery guy arrives at the door yet again. And now you're 0 for 3—you're out! Another set of New Year's resolutions goes down in flames, and you descend into a shame spiral, pint of ice cream firmly in hand.

Awful, isn't it? We've all been there, and we would all prefer not to go there again. But using design in your life bypasses this self-defeating process, and it is an especially effective way to take charge of your health and wellness.

The first step in designing anything in your life is to realize that although past attempts haven't worked out, that doesn't mean you failed. Nothing could be further from the truth. It simply means that you unconsciously judged yourself into a state of defeat. When your first effort didn't work, you thought it meant you were done, and you checked the Failed box next to that goal. But what if you just step back and figure out what the next version of your design might be, the version that improves upon the obstacles and design flaws found in the last version? You would be thinking like a designer. A designer mindset means that there is no failure—there is only the latest release version (like the iPhone 4, 5, 6, etc.). To this way of thinking, a design is never finished and you are never a failure.

This is where it's important to understand the real power of designing your life. Successful designers— think architects, fashion designers, engineers—don't create just one sketch and leave it at that. They use their original idea as a starting point. They rethink it and make lots of adjustments. They tinker. They build a model and experiment to see what works and what doesn't. The final building, garment, or system is likely to be vastly different from the original drawing, but the designer doesn't call that first effort a failure. It was simply a version, an iteration, or a mock-up. Wonderfully nonjudgmental terms, aren't they? Quite refreshing and forgiving compared to the words we normally use to describe our own efforts.

Designing something in your life is no different. The initial blueprint is never the final version. If we think of our designs as fluid entities that we expect to tweak and adjust as we go along, we have a much better chance of working around the habenula's failure count. We can fly below our judgmental, self-defeating, all-or-nothing radar! Steering around this part of our brain, we make ourselves immune to failure because we define ourselves not by a win-lose record, but by the fact that we're evolving. We're trying, we're practicing, we're designing—and that's really all we have to do.

Do you see how powerful that concept is? When something doesn't work out the way you want it to, the flaw was in the design, not in you. Instead of calling it a failure and giving up, you call it a design and keep going.

This is good news. This is fixable. This is your ticket to freedom, and you can finally pull that stake out of the ground with all that power you didn't realize you had!

ANOTHER COUNTER IN YOUR BRAIN

One of the most intriguing health conversations I ever had was during a stress-reduction workshop I was leading. The participants were a diverse group of service providers, such as nurses, teachers, youth workers, and physicians. I asked each of them to describe a time when they were at their healthiest. A young woman who worked as a tutor for an after-school program gushed about her health kick last year—she was eating right, doing yoga, and biking to work every day. She beamed as she went on and on about how good she felt during that time. I was curious what had caused her to stop when she had obviously felt so much better.

"So... what happened?" I asked.

Her face went blank, her eyes searching for an answer.

"I don't know," she replied.

She truly had no idea why she was unable to maintain the healthy habits that made her feel so good. And why does that qualify as one of my most intriguing health conversations? Because it was the first time I was exposed to a very powerful driver of our behaviors—our intrinsic memory system.

While the habenula keeps a running count of our failures, our intrinsic memory system counts patterns that we cannot consciously track. It's a numbers game. Our senses transmit 11 million bits per second to our brain for processing, but our conscious mind only processes 50 bits per second.[7] Enter the intrinsic memory system. This part of our unconscious mind secretly tracks patterns behind the scenes, even altering our behavior before we know that we have changed our behavior, or changed our mind, or even why we did. There are famous psychology experiments involving blue and red card decks that demonstrate how those playing with the cards were observed to change which cards they were selecting before they knew it. And even when they knew they were favoring one card deck over the other, it took a while for them to consciously know why.[8]

I once found myself repeatedly canceling plans with someone who had long been a close friend. We hadn't had an argument and there seemed to be no reason for my behavior, and yet I was routinely avoiding spending time with her without knowing why. When I became aware of the pattern, I suddenly realized that I no longer enjoyed her company because she judged everything I did, from my clothing to my parenting choices. I was also reminded that earlier that year, I had set a conscious intention to surround myself with supportive, loving people, so that I could stop wasting my energy on unhealthy relationships. Our fading friendship wasn't me being flaky, as it first appeared to be, but was actually the result of my own self-induced behavior design—it's just that my intrinsic memory put two and two together before I consciously did. Our intrinsic memory system is a powerful force, and it is always one or more steps ahead of our conscious awareness.

A well-meaning dietician I know wanted to drink more water daily in order to inspire her patients with diabetes. So she filled a one-gallon jug every morning with the goal of drinking it throughout the day. She proudly told me about her design. But after two weeks she found that she was not finishing it as planned, and was, in fact, drinking less and less with each passing day.

In talking with her, I found that she was still committed and enthusiastic about her goal, but when I probed a little deeper, she revealed that she was feeling frustrated that she was failing at it. When asked why, she didn't seem to know why she had stopped finishing the water. Sound familiar? "I guess I just keep forgetting to drink it," she said. I disagreed and told her that something about her design was not working for her or else she would be doing it successfully. When we explored her unconscious experience of the one-gallon jug system, we uncovered the real reason she was drinking less: she felt guilty for taking so many bathroom breaks throughout her workday.

I worked with her to design her next version, using a smaller bottle and planned bathroom breaks, and she resumed her practice of drinking more water. Notice how her intrinsic memory system had picked up on the flaws in her original one-gallon design and was causing her to change her behavior before she could consciously tell me what was happening.

But just as your intrinsic memory system helps and protects you, it can also work against your good intentions and efforts. January 1 rolls around and you are pumped up with motivation. Seizing the moment, you ambitiously go on a highly restrictive diet. On the surface, you are eating healthy and losing weight. But lurking beneath all of this progress is your intrinsic memory secretly tallying up all that deprivation you feel as you pass on the cupcakes at work, all your disappointment at not having a glass of wine with your friends, and all the anger that you feel because you have to make all these sacrifices while everyone else is enjoying themselves! Inevitably, this is where the rebellion starts brewing deep down inside you. It's not fair, it's hard, and you shouldn't have to be so miserable just to lose a few pounds. You start to see old behaviors breaking through—a little cheating here, then there, then twice on Sunday. Hello Relapse, my old friend. The rubber band has been stretched too far, and it snaps you right back into your old eating habits. Oh, crap!

How does this change if we use design instead? First, you don't expect to succeed; you expect to tinker. Second, you know better than to start with a rigid, harsh design because you don't want to set off your intrinsic memory system, which only wants to protect you from such suffering. Third, whenever you see your behavior reverting to old patterns, you just speak softly to your habenula and say "Hey, don't count this as a failure. This is totally normal! It is just a signal telling me to update my design."

For example, let's say you keep meaning to go to the gym before work, but you never seem to make it. Fine. No biggie. You simply look at the evidence (Ahem, the fact that you aren't actually doing what you intended!) and you know that your first version design needs tweaking. Don't judge it, just iterate on it. There are lots of design options you can use to help you get there. Maybe you try putting your alarm clock across the room because you have a wicked snooze button habit. Or maybe you pack your gym bag in advance and put it right by the front door the night before because you tend to run late in the morning. Or perhaps you commit to meeting a trusted friend for an early spin class because when you were in high school you had fun exercising with your friends, and you know that you get lonely or lazy when you try to work out alone. In other words, only you know how to catch you. Only you know what you will try to wriggle out of, and only you know what you will rebel against. So you create the design that is perfect for you; you finally get to the gym, and you feel like a superstar all day. Success!

But what if even that starts to break down? A week goes by and you're hitting the snooze bar again, staying in bed, or stepping right over the packed gym bag as you leave the house. That's totally OK. It's just time for a redesign. Rather than aiming for an early morning workout, maybe now you try a post-dinner walk around the neighborhood or sign up for a lunchtime yoga class. Or maybe you put some weights or a sturdy stool next to the couch and try to exercise while you watch TV. If you think of your design as fluid and subject to change, you never fail. You're simply working on your next iteration. It's almost like your past self is constantly plotting to capture the attention and enlist the effort of your future self without inciting a rebellion. This is something that we'll design for in chapter 8.

WE ALL DESIGN, WE JUST DON'T KNOW IT

I learned a lot about designing life from my mom. She was a single mother supporting two children on about $11,000 a year, but, boy, she was an expert at designing a life that worked. She combed yard sales and thrift stores for furniture and household items, tastefully decorating our rural home on the cheap. She couldn't afford to buy us the expensive brand name jeans that defined us as teenagers then, so she ingeniously replaced our humble jean labels with designer ones. Her designs helped us fit in with our more affluent friends. Brilliant! Rather than being paralyzed by her circumstances, Mom continually tweaked her designs and succeeded in building a beautiful, quality life for our family. She always said she should have been an interior decorator, but in reality, she was much more than a decorator. She was a scrappy DIY designer of life, and she shared that gift with us kids.

You're probably already designing your life in small ways without even realizing it. When you're taking an antibiotic, you leave the bottle on the counter so you'll remember to continue taking it even after you begin to feel better. You have a tray for your keys right by the door so you don't misplace them. You keep your driver's license and the cards you use most often in the front part of your wallet, and you keep your reusable grocery bags in the car so you won't forget them when you go to the store. You may think you are just being methodical, but when you inherently do this with simple things, you are employing design. My point is that this same natural skill can be expanded and intentionally applied to just about anything you want to change.

ALL DESIGNS EXPIRE

Be aware that even when you find a design that works, it's always subject to change. Nothing in life is permanent, so expect that every one of your designs comes with an expiration date. For example, you are probably not still wearing the same clothes you did in high school, right? You knew when it was time to update your look (unless you're my dad, who has a permanent jeans and hoodie look going on). The big mystery in implementing your design is that the expiration date isn't printed on the package, so you might not see it coming. You've always stayed in shape by running, but now your knees have had enough. You're devastated by the sudden loss of a loved one and mashed potatoes suddenly offer a helpful coping mechanism. Your income drops and that gym membership is a luxury you can no longer afford. All of these circumstances can instantly sour a design that was working for you.

Most designs expire slowly and silently, though. Just as the after-school tutor mysteriously went from the healthiest year of her life to "what the heck happened to my good habits?!," most people don't see the signs of their designs expiring. Recognizing the signs is easy if we know what to look for. Our favorite, New Year's resolutions, provides the perfect example, yet again.

On January 2, I look around my neighborhood and there are people jogging past my house. At five in the morning! In the cold! They're out of shape, out of breath, and destined for sore muscles, but there they are anyway. I watch them pass and say to myself, "Go, people! You can do it!" When I get to the gym, the parking lot is packed, the place is filled with people I've never seen before, and the guy at the front desk is busy signing up new members. My city is suddenly full of people who are happily implementing a new design for improving their health. Good for them!

The change comes gradually. The joggers skip a day, then another, then a week, and soon they just snuggle deeper into the covers and go back to sleep. The gym parking lot becomes emptier day by day, and eventually I have my choice of treadmills again. The newly minted joggers and gym rats had set firm goals for themselves, but then their intrinsic memory system kicked in, reminding them of how unpleasant this all is and how much easier life was before all this early morning gym nonsense. Their health design silently hits its expiration date, goes bad, and gets thrown out like sour milk. The habenula chalks another one up to failure. And if you ask them what happened, they won't know why, exactly, they stopped, just like the dietician not finishing her gallon jug of water or the after-school tutor who stopped doing yoga.

When I speak to groups on this topic, I often show a short video that perfectly illustrates the concept of thinking like a designer so that you can always recover. A seven-year-old boy is alone on a baseball field. He looks to the sky and yells, "I'm the greatest hitter in the world!" But when he throws the ball into the air and swings at it, he misses entirely. Strike one. Again he yells, "I'm the greatest hitter in the world!" and misses. He examines his bat—nope, no holes there—before taking a big swing. Strike two. Undeterred, he adjusts his cap, once more yells, "I'm the greatest hitter in the world," and with a determined look worthy of a major leaguer, gives it his all. Strike three. After considering his situation for a moment (while his habenula raises the ugly specter of failure), he suddenly breaks into a huge grin, looks up and happily yells, "I'm the greatest pitcher in the world!" He has successfully iterated his design, so he can keep going, improving, and playing his game.

By now, you are seeing the choice you face. Either stick with what you've been doing, setting rigid goals and gambling on hard wins and losses, or start thinking of everything as a design, with multiple iterations that lead to the life you want. For many of us, the hardest thing to let go of when making this choice is our dysfunctional acceptance of our own self-judgment. Oddly enough, unconsciously, most of us stay in our abusive relationship with our negative self-talk, forever chained to that stake in the ground, accepting the powerless baby elephant in our minds. As unhealthy as it is to stick with the status quo, it is very comfortable and known. (Don't worry; we will deal with this in the next chapter.)

You wouldn't think you were a bad person because you stopped wearing a sweater you bought and loved wearing a decade ago, and yet why do you think you are bad just because you got tired of those early morning workouts?

Using design is our ticket out of such neurosis. It helps make changing our life as normal as changing our sweater. It is our way to be with what we know is true: our lives are dynamic, we are never the same, and unpredictable, unspoken needs constantly arise. Design gives us the excuse we need to shush our self-judgment, the ability to muster our optimism to try again, and the creativity to iterate our way right into the results we need to change our lives for the better.

Notes

②

compassion is king and queen

My mind is a bad neighborhood
I try not to go into alone.

— Anne Lamott

absolutely adored my friend, Huong, whom I met in medical school. She was bold and smart and loving. I wanted her to like me just so I could bask in her radiance. So, imagine my surprise one day when we were hanging out with a group of friends, joking around, and she called me out. I was 28 at the time.

I had made a joke about one of our other friends, teasing her about her absentmindedness. Huong spoke firmly and bluntly to me at that moment. She told me that it was uncomfortable to be around me because she found me very critical. She reflected back to me that when I made jokes that I thought were funny, they had a bite to them, kind of mocking or making light of something that was missing in a person.

I was so ashamed.

Here was my dear friend, whom I desperately wanted to approve of me, telling me that I was not pleasant to be around! This really gave me pause. I had never realized that my dark humor was hurting people. In my family, this was normal. I didn't know how to reply to her. It was too painful for me at that moment to ask her to say more so that I could learn from my mistakes. Instead, I curled up into a little ball on the couch and remained quiet for the rest of the evening—then I went home and cried.

About two years later, around my 30th birthday, I took a stroll on a Saturday that changed my life. In those days, to reduce the intense stress of my life I had made a practice of taking slow, contemplative walks in nature. I would ask my then husband to watch our two- and four-year-old daughters while I walked to a nearby wooded area to reconnect with myself. On this one particular walk, I found myself wandering into a new area I had not explored before. In front of me, a low-hanging branch of a young tree rocked in the gentle breeze. At eye level I noticed a teeny tiny woven basket stuck to the tree: a hummingbird nest! Now, if you've never seen one of these, they are ridiculously cute! Hummingbirds are like nature's miniature basket-weaving artisans, who could take their itty-bitty baskets to the bird community's farmers market and sell them on weekends.

Of course, the cuteness of that teacup nest was so potent that before I knew it, a tear had formed in the corner of my eye and had run down my face. I decided to sit down right under that tree to honor this gift of beauty from the universe. Then the memory of Huong calling me out flashed in my mind and I cringed with shame—the memory and emotions as freshly preserved as if it had happened yesterday.

Why did I still cringe at this when it happened years ago? To further explore this question, I willfully summoned other painful memories of times and behaviors I was not proud of. Lies I had told, gossip I had spread, and codependence I had invited. Each one delivered a sting of unresolved emotions and unhealed shame. I could barely stand it. I felt powerful urges to justify my actions, to deny that it was as bad as it was, to blame the other people in the story. I could sense the contracture of my defense mechanisms. I had to do something to prevent closing up again.

Instinctively, I sat in silence in a sort of meditative state. In my mind, I prayed to heal from the weight of all of this shame that seemed perfectly frozen in intensity, unthawed by the passing of time. As a sort of playful, curious thought experiment, I pictured myself hovering above and looking down at myself. I focused on looking upon my current self in a loving way, much like a gentle mother who was seeing me through the eyes of compassion. Then I again called up each painful memory, starting in my early childhood. One by one, moving forward in time, I looked at the role that I had played in each shameful situation—when I had lied or had done something embarrassing, when I had reacted in anger, when I had disappointed myself, when I had not stood up for myself.

I envisioned hovering over my five-year-old self and saying, "I forgive you for being too young and scared to really stand up to your parents when they were criticizing you."

To my eight-year-old self, I said, "I forgive you for being too prideful and scared to tell the truth."

To my sixteen-year-old self, I said, "I forgive you for

being addicted to fast food in high school because you were depressed and unable to find another solution to feel better."

Fast forward: "I forgive you for being so insecure that you put that other person down." And then, "I forgive you for being too scared to stand up for that patient and just going along with the way that she was treated."

Tears were streaming down my face. For at least 90 minutes if not longer, there I sat going through the inventory of my ugliest, most cowardly and disappointing actions, and for the first time choosing to look upon myself with compassion and forgiving myself systematically.

I noticed something incredible after that day. I could hear feedback better. I could be more curious about how I was affecting other people because I wasn't busy defending myself. If I accidentally hurt someone, I no longer had to run away or deny it out of the pain of observing and owning my actions. The tearful experience in the woods that day had given me the fortitude to sit with how I can do awful things and yet still love myself, how I can still care for myself even when I sink to my lowest, least evolved behaviors.

A DESIGNER'S FIRST STEP IS COMPASSION

Here's the mindset I would wish upon you if I had the power: "Hey, I'm not perfect but I *can* design using that imperfection." I want you to see your imperfection, even your shame, as a design project. As a designer of your life, you are not designing for perfection; you are designing for healing, for improvement, for empowerment. I want you to have compassion for yourself. This is your first step as a designer. It is how you start every day when building the life that you want for yourself.

Now that you understand the promise of designing to improve your life, you may be tempted to jump right in and start designing. And if you are designing something totally benign, like how to organize the silverware for easy access, that's just fine. But most of the things we really want to change in our life are loaded with emotion—our own or others. For these areas, if we only focus on the pragmatic physical aspect of the design, it may lead to disaster—sabotage, rebellion, resistance. Before we draft behavioral blueprints to design the life we want for any areas loaded with emotional landmines, we need to first talk about compassion.

IDEO, a leading global design firm, emphasizes starting each design with empathy. Empathy is defined on www.dictionary.com as experiencing the feelings, thoughts, or attitudes of another. I have been privileged to learn of IDEO's signature design thinking process, which also fuels the foundation for the Stanford d.school (design school), from one of its early founders, Dennis Boyle. Regardless of what they are making, which spans a wide array of products—soaps, kitchen utensils, bicycles, medical devices, health apps, etc., IDEO designers are trained to first and foremost understand the world through their customers' eyes. Their design thinking discipline of listening and empathy before they design has made the designers at IDEO some of the greatest creative leaders of our time.

Empathy must also be the first step when you are designing for behavioral change. Why is this? Two reasons. First, if you are designing for your family, like the fridge design I described in the previous chapter, you want to really understand how your family members feel. Had I dictated to my kids, made them feel guilty about eating junk food, and stomped on their body image, my design would have caused emotional injury to their self-esteem as well as our relationship. Likewise, had I just manipulated them like puppets without empathy for their experience and needs, they would have rebelled or rejected my efforts. Second, if you are designing for your own behavior, it can get even more intense. Just like my walk in the forest, we can all happen upon pain points and unresolved grief that underpin the very behaviors we are trying to change. In a way, when I am designing for myself, I am two people: the designer and the client of the designer. And if I go about the process as an aggressive, insensitive a-hole designer, my client would naturally want to fire me. A common adage in psychology is that if someone actually spoke to us the way we speak to ourselves silently in our head, we would never be friends with them. Empathy helps us be effective and helps our designs to be relevant and not harmful. And, I would add, empathy does not go far enough.

As we design change in our lives, we inevitably stumble upon things that are really hard to look at—ugly, humbling, hateful things. We may have deceived or broken trust with other people; we may have disappointed and broken trust with ourselves. Basically, everything we would choose or want to change about our lives is being held in place by some form of defense mechanism. Therefore, when we attempt to change, we break the seal on the negative emotion we were trying to avoid. Like my critical humor that Huong pointed out, there are habits we each develop that have helped us survive. They are embarrassing to face and even more terrifying to release.

In these moments, compassion must be used because empathy alone would be overwhelming. If I have never touched within myself the true emotions beneath my bad habits (whether I'm addicted to smoking, shopping, or potato chips), empathy only helps me understand why I am doing it and how I am feeling about it—but I may still be stuck feeling horrible. It is not enough to understand that I feel completely alone if no one cares.

Compassion solves this. It goes beyond empathy. Compassion summons deep sympathy plus the desire to alleviate suffering. In this state of mind, I want to care for myself. Compassion compels me to take action on my own behalf.

THE DIFFERENCE BETWEEN EMPATHY AND COMPASSION

Powerful evidence of this comes out of neuroscience. Researchers have shown that distinct areas of the brain (for my fellow geeks: the secondary somatosensory cortex and the insular cortex) become active when we are exposed to suffering in another person. One significant brain scan (fMRI) study[9] demonstrated that there are, in fact, different brain areas associated with an empathetic response and a compassionate response. People who were trained in a special method of developing compassion called loving-kindness meditation showed enhanced activity in the temporoparietal junction, the medial prefrontal cortex, and the superior temporal sulcus, which is a multi-sensory area that gets activated when listening to voices or attending to where another person's gaze is (i.e., related to social interactions with other people). However, these study participants also had years of meditation practice, so researchers wondered if the same is true for normal everyday people.

A few years later, another brain scan study[10] examined the differences between empathy and compassion and the degree to which these traits are enhanced by training normal everyday people who had never meditated. In this study, the researchers divided the study participants into two groups. One group received compassion training while the other group was trained in empathy for others. After just a week of training, individuals in both groups watched videos of people who were suffering. The compassion-trained individuals reported more benevolence and even positive feelings when viewing the videos. In contrast, the empathy-trained individuals were troubled by negative feelings and thoughts—sometimes to the point that they could not contain their distressing emotions and became quite upset. The conclusion? Empathy in the absence of compassion can lead to burnout, a condition that impacts many caregivers, first-responders, and clinicians as a sort of empathy fatigue.

And there's more. The researchers then gave the empathy group the compassion training. When these people were retested with more videos of suffering, the troubling effect of the empathy-only training improved; the group reported fewer negative emotions and more positive and caring emotions. Moreover, these self-reported emotional experiences corresponded with changes in several areas of the brain (including the orbitofrontal cortex, the ventral striatum, and the anterior cingulate cortex, which is known to play a key role in emotional aspects of decision-making and behavioral consequences such as anticipating rewards and evaluating errors).

The take-home message here is clear. Recognizing suffering and understanding what we feel is not enough. There has to be a genuine desire to stop the suffering.

Compassion does this. Compassion is like Empathy 2.0. The designer in you must approach the design client in you with a tremendous amount of compassion in order to be effective.

COMPASSION AS MEDICINE

One act of compassion I will never forget came as a surprise on a hectic, stressful morning before work. My eleven-year-old daughter had awakened that morning with a fever and likely ear infection. At this point in my life, I was a single mother holding down an executive leadership role at a large healthcare company. This particular morning just happened to be the day of my high-stakes, cannot-possibly-miss pitch meeting for our wellness division. The deal was worth multiple millions and I was the main designer on the project. No one could substitute for me; I had to make it! With all of my heart, I wanted to stay home and take care of my daughter. But, in reality, I knew that it would cause irreversible damage to my leadership role if I didn't make the meeting. And my daughter was not in danger because of her illness. She just needed to see a doctor some time that day.

I called the nurse line to try to schedule an urgent care appointment for her. The nurse listened to my plight but told me she didn't have any appointments. Feeling like the worst mother on the planet and fearful of the nurse's judgment, I asked her whether I could give my daughter Tylenol to break her fever just enough to get her to school. I then could fetch her as soon as I could after my meeting. The nurse was reluctant to endorse my plan because we both knew that sending a feverish child to school is against policy, but she said that it would work to get us into an afternoon slot they had open.

My stomach churned with guilt as I made plans to leave my sick daughter. It was an impossible situation with no good solution—a dilemma I'm sure most working parents have faced at some point or another. Done with scheduling, I was about to hang up the phone when the nurse took me by surprise.

"You know, I really hope your daughter feels better."

"Oh my god, thank you!" I was taken aback.

I cannot tell you how many nurses or healthcare workers with whom I have interacted are terse, grumpy, or judgmental. It's definitely a stressful job! One hero of mine, Stanford neurosurgeon Dr. Jim Doty, has created the Center for Compassion and Altruism Research and Education (CCARE), which studies the science of compassion and trains healthcare and business professionals in how to practice it. The center teaches clinicians to respond like this nurse—her comment streaming right from her heart, touching mine instantly. She alleviated my intense suffering with the tiniest dose of compassion. Conversely, when someone judges us, all our defenses fly up and we brace for impact. Each of us, no matter how tough our exterior, experiences this.

The same is true if you are that other person to yourself. Having compassion for yourself will help you relax. Judging yourself will put you in a state of anxiety and mistrust. Easy to say, harder to fix. How can you practice compassion for yourself when the biggest opponent to this is your negative self-talk, which plays constantly but quietly in the background as you go about your day?

HAND TO HEART

A friend of mine illustrated for me how to have compassion for ourselves whenever we need it. She had gone to stay at a monastery after the sudden loss of her fiancé. Filled with pain and grief, she expected to find peace. Instead, she found the slow, deliberate pace and silent monastic environment to be almost maddening. Rather than the bustle of San Francisco that distracted her constantly, in the monastery she had nothing but herself and her grieving thoughts. Day in and day out, everything she did, whether dishes or meditation, was accompanied by intense emotions and thoughts of her beloved's death. What's worse, an unresolved childhood trauma as well as losing her mother when she was twelve started to kick up in unexpected ways. She would be in the midst of doing laundry and suddenly be struck by overwhelming grief. It was so strong that she often couldn't catch her breath. Even sobbing would be unstoppable for hours.

But she found a way to tap her self-compassion. She wrote me a letter describing what she had been experiencing: "Sometimes, when I cannot see for the tears in my eyes, and I cannot inhale to cry out even one more time, I simply put my arms around my body. I hold on to myself, repeating, *'I'm here for you. I'm here for you.'*"

How tender! How loving! Imagine how comforting it would feel for another person to sit with you during your darkest times and repeat gently, "I'm here for you." Most of us do not realize that it works just as powerfully if we do this for ourselves. I would argue that this is perhaps more powerful since we are invoking our own self-reliance rather than relying on things outside of ourselves to cure us. We can be our own designer!

Soon after receiving my friend's letter, I joined a month-long retreat on compassion. Similarly, in the silence and contemplative practice, I went through strong waves of emotion that at times seemed like they would never end. I sought the advice of my instructor, Sylvia, one of the most compassionate people I have ever known. She suggested that I hold my hand on my heart whenever I felt overwhelmed. I felt a little self-conscious at first, but in actual practice it started to feel natural fairly quickly. And it really worked! I have since used this technique in my workshops, and people love how easy and effective it is to help us connect immediately to and cultivate compassion for ourselves.

SELF-DEFENSES

One area I defended as a younger woman was my tough demeanor. My dad was raised in a harsh environment. His dad was a farmer and my dad once watched him beat a bull with a tire chain—makes me shudder just thinking of it. Although he buffered much of it, inevitably my dad passed some of that harshness onto me. He thought that tough love would make me tough. And it did. It cut me off from my heart for years.

By the time I got to medical school, I was hardcore too. I wanted to go into surgery—not because I was primarily motivated to help people, but because I was extremely competitive, even wanting to cure cancer so I could get a Nobel Prize. My aspirations were very academic, cerebral, and ego-driven.

Luckily, I also got involved with volunteering in the community. I worked at the free clinic with homeless patients. I started to serve elderly patients in their home. I also taught medical education to disadvantaged youth that were incarcerated in juvenile hall. These young people, whom society feared, were particularly endearing to me—they were really wonderful kids most of the time, who had done a few really horrific things. In getting to know them, I saw that their negative choices and actions were really just oozing out of the abscesses of their childhood abuse and neglect. They didn't know what it was like to be on the receiving end of compassion, and that's how they got to where they were. As one of my wise elders, who is Native American, once said, "Hurt people hurt people." In many ways, they were not unlike me—raised by the adage of suck it up, which offers little compassion for suffering. Through service to others, I started to soften. I opened my heart, which

I had closed off years before because I was trying to be tough and strong.

Whatever is negative inside us will not only hurt us, it will leak out as toxins to those around us as well. My habit of criticizing, which Huong pointed out, was simply a symptom of what was inside me—I was a hardened person who defended herself against the world around her. At the same time, all of my community service and the connections I experienced with others helped cultivate an outward-facing compassion that eventually came back to me when I took that walk in the woods and sat under the hummingbird's nest.

Hand on Heart Practice

Try this self-compassion exercise whenever you are experiencing strong emotion:

Place your hand over your heart. Take a few deep, slow breaths. Your heartbeat has carried you through all of your life experiences, both good and bad, to bring you to where you are today. Can you attune to the sensations in your chest from your beating heart? Can you feel the warmth of your hand? If your hand is touching your shirt, what does that fabric feel like? If your hand is on your skin, what does that feel like? Can you feel your heartbeat? Can you notice your breathing pattern?

Dive down into the sensation as finely as you can. Just feel what it feels like to connect to yourself, to stabilize and comfort yourself. Through this gesture of your hand connecting with your heart, repeat, "I'm here for you." You are here for yourself. This is medici you can use at any time.

SEP 2 6 2017

You can do this hand-on-heart exercise whenever needed to give yourself a sense of being grounded and as a reminder that there will be an end to the suffering you're currently feeling. You can do this when you're driving, watching TV, in a meeting (no kidding!)—whenever you need it. You can do it in stealth mode if you're out in public by crossing your arms with the one tucked in your armpit or playing with your necklace—no one knows what you're doing but you! You can make it a very natural-looking position or gesture.

This simple contact with your own heart can help you get through the intensity of an experience without shutting down. It's a tool to instantly connect with your compassion for yourself as you start to design new behaviors.

As you start to change your own behaviors, designing to improve them, you can expect to stumble upon some surprising and maybe highly protected areas of your ego self. It's a normal part of the process. In that moment when we look upon what we are not proud of, we can be thankful to ourselves for surviving the hardship by putting up those protections. We can celebrate our resiliency.

In that moment, we can also learn to hold onto ourselves and say, "I'm here for you, dear one, and it's OK to let go of this." We can forgive ourselves for the binge eating, the conflict avoidance, the gossiping as a way to vent, the codependency—whatever we use as our go-to defense. Designing new behaviors for yourself is guaranteed to trigger your self-protection as a consequence of hitting something really important to iterate and improve upon. That's the heart of it all.

Self-compassion is every behavior designer's salve—and it is the primary substrate that will help you move through the changes you are creating!

Notes

3

fast brain, slow brain

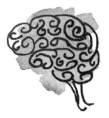

*Happiness is when what you think, what you say,
and what you do are in harmony.*

—Mahatma Gandhi

While serving as a medical director in a large health-care organization, I was running a clinical study on metabolic syndrome in collaboration with Duke University and an online classroom company, eMindful. The study involved several hundred volunteers going through weekly lessons to help them lose weight and reverse their risk of heart disease and diabetes. I had the chance to talk to some of them about their experience in the program—to see how it was working. One woman, Lisa, a successful saleswoman in her mid-40s, especially loved the experience and started raving about the program.

"Wow, ya know, I'm just learning so much! I know what to eat, in what order, how to eat slowly." She beamed about the specific tips and exercises that had clicked with her and the behaviors that she had changed. Then she paused, her face softened to seriousness and her eyes searched mine.

"But, the thing is... I know what I *should* do—I just don't know why I don't do it."

This simple truth knocked me out of my interviewer seat for a moment while I pondered what she said.

That's it! I thought, *That's why we don't change!*

But, what was the *it*? What is it that prevents Lisa and all of us from doing what we know we should do, or even what we really, really want to do—for our health— or for our life?

Ever since I can remember I have been asking this question. As a child, I pondered why adults would say, "these things will kill me" as they took another drag off their cigarette. As a teenager, I counted the number of diets my mother tried, watching her lose weight then gain it back. As a college student, I watched myself help- lessly go back to that loser ex-boyfriend who I knew was not good for me. As a mentor to gang youth, I saw them return to the streets even after swearing they were going to change. And as a physician, I watched my patients fail over and over again in their attempts to change their lifestyle, even after a major, painful event that was certain to be their wake-up call. It wasn't a matter of sincerity, because in all cases I knew that each of these people wanted to be free—they just didn't know why they couldn't do it!.

From the moment I heard it, "I know what I should do, I don't know why I don't do it" became my one-pointed mantra and the mystery I needed to solve—for myself and for everyone else.

THE GAP

We all do things that we know we shouldn't. And we all neglect to do things that we know we should. Illogically, these backward patterns fly in the face of our best intentions. We can be an enigma even to ourselves. The answers to designing and changing our behavior lie in this gap between what we know we should do and what we actually do. Lisa's words focused my attention squarely on this gap. I knew that if I could understand it—map out the unknown terrain that separates our intentions from our actions—I could help people solve important problems and live how they truly want to live.

My understanding of this gap has accrued over many years. I had experiences with it as a professional trying to help people and as an academic trying to learn the science behind it. But perhaps my most powerful lesson was when I was dipping in and out of this gap as a frustrated patient in what became a decade-long medical mystery.

In 2001, I came down with a nasty case of food poisoning. Truthfully, I kind of deserved it because I had become addicted to fresh mozzarella cheese balls, which I had started to eat by the tub most days after work. Alas, my gluttony was punished as I consumed a tainted tub of mozzarella, which landed me in bed for four days, losing so much fluid that my dear surgeon friend came to the house with an IV bag to rehydrate me. I recovered and life went on. But I was not the same.

Over the next year, my life reached peak levels of stress as I went through a divorce. I felt tired all the time. Uncontrollably tired. My evening commute turned into a death-defying daily feat as I was literally falling asleep at the wheel. What was worse, I would get home and make dinner for my young daughters, four- and six-years-old at the time, only to pass out inexplicably for hours right afterward. I would wake up in a panic. "Oh my god! Where are my kids?! What happened?!" Thankfully, I would find them playing quietly with their dolls, but it terrified me to think I had left them unsupervised for hours. These sleeping episodes were deep and sudden as if someone had drugged me. I rationalized that it was just high stress.

But it didn't get better. Four years later, after de-stressing my life and changing my environment, I was still falling asleep without warning. After many design efforts to heal my fatigue, I finally went to a Western doctor. She thought I had allergies. I never had allergies before and my symptoms were not consistent with environmental or seasonal allergens, so I begged to disagree. I left her office, discouraged and at my wit's end, six years of frustrating medical mystery and no solution in sight.

Driving home from my appointment, I was at a stoplight when a dialog erupted in my head.

"Allergies. Come on. I don't have allergies."

Then an intuitive reply, "Don't be so sure. It may not be in the air or environment. It may be something you are eating."

Then me again, "Well, I have heard of these weird

diets where people are dairy- and wheat-free. Maybe I will try that?"

So, scientifically, I conducted a design experiment on myself and removed all dairy and wheat from my diet. Shockingly, three days later, I was back! No more passing out! I sprung back to life and reclaimed *me*—the one with boundless energy that everyone used to know. I was my old self again!

Soon after making this discovery, I was discussing my case with a gastroenterologist at a friend's dinner party. He confirmed my findings, describing that some of his patients developed antibodies to specific foods, which then caused an allergy. We hypothesized that my tainted mozzarella binge and resulting food poisoning had left me with an allergy to milk protein and whey.

Now I had my explanation. It fit my symptoms. The sleepiness followed eating milk products, but also followed eating processed foods that had whey as a flavor additive, which had made it trickier to decipher a cause and effect pattern. Perhaps, after so many years, my intrinsic memory system had finally tracked the pattern and was trying to get through to my conscious mind. After so many years living in a body that didn't feel like my own, I finally felt free.

Now that I knew what I should do, I was all set, right? Hardly!

The problem was two words: *ice cream.*

I loved ice cream. I had zero control over my craving for it. If ice cream was in the house or on the menu, it was going into my mouth. Now that I knew I had a dairy allergy, I knew I shouldn't eat ice cream. But I still wanted to eat ice cream. And that's where the gap began.

Here's how it went. I would be out on a date, have ice cream for dessert—despite knowing what would happen—and fall asleep riding in the car on the way home. I would be at a birthday party for my daughter's friend and, of course, would have to have ice cream with my cake! A few hours later, the hostess would be waking me from her couch because everyone had left but us. And the absolute worst: on a car trip to my dad's, I had a sundae at a truck stop along the way and couldn't wake up until noon the next day, like a hungover teenager. My farm-raised dad, who is up predawn, greeted me with "well, good morning" in a snarky, you-lazy-ass tone. Of course, I never ever ate dairy when I was alone with my girls because it was a safety risk, but the rest of the time my temptations overcame me, regardless of the consequence.

I was the epitome of someone living in the gap between what I knew I should do and what I kept doing. It was as though I resembled the cartoon character Homer Simpson. Homer, despite his best intentions to avoid doing bad things, always ends up impulsively doing them. Then after he realizes what he has done, he blurts out "D'oh." I kept having that D'oh moment—but then I'd do it all over again. Why was this happening?

All I knew was that I had a logical, planning part of me and an impulsive, forgetful, and devil-may-care part of me. In this gap existed all of my frustrations with myself, my shame for not doing what I should, and my disappointment for not making progress. Over time, the negative, and consequential, feedback loop between my eating dairy and falling asleep slowly closed this gap (slowly, as in it took another five years!). I noticed a longer and longer stretch of time in between each ice cream binge and fewer and fewer spoonfuls each time.

WE HAVE TWO BRAINS, FAST AND SLOW

A few years later I learned why this gap was happening to me—and so many other people. As a neuroscience hobbyist, it was my practice to read everything I could on human (and animal) behavior patterns. I was hungry to figure out the "I know what to do, I don't know why I don't do it" gap.

One of the most significant pieces of the puzzle came from Daniel Kahneman's book *Thinking, Fast and Slow*,[11] based on his Nobel Prize-winning discoveries in economic behavioral sciences. Dr. Kahneman describes two modes of thought that psychologists call system 1 and system 2. System 1 represents the fast, instinctual, and emotional mind. It takes shortcuts, makes quick judgments, generates rough estimates, and creates mindless habits. Our system 2 way of thinking, in contrast, is all about being slow and deliberate. In this mode, we apply logic, carefully calculate answers, and make goals, plans, and strategies.

When I teach workshops in designing for behavior change, I find it easier for everyone if we don't have to keep remembering which one is system 1 and which one is system 2. As a mental shortcut, I have found that renaming system 1 the fast brain and system 2 the slow brain helps people apply the concepts more easily. Therefore, as an imperfect metaphor, I am going to use the term *fast brain* to represent system 1 and *slow brain* to represent system 2.

The fast brain represents our unconscious mind, where we tuck away habitual ways of being so that we do not have to figure it out anew every time we need to drive home from work, for instance. It is our auto-pilot. Researchers estimate that our sensory nerves fire off 11 million sensory inputs per second to our brain. We cannot possibly focus on every one of these inputs *and* carefully process them all. So, what do we do? Our fast brain comes to our rescue, helping us distill much of this into rules of thumb, common sense, and habits. It saves our slow brain effort for solving novel problems and making decisions. The fast brain helps us cope with our complex world by giving us the tools to ignore what we can. And as our technology-based world speeds us up and we get even more stimulated, our fast brain tends to dominate our actions to keep us from becoming overwhelmed. The fast brain, as our unconscious mind, has been estimated to drive 95 percent of our behavior,[12] like ice cream-eating behavior.

Now, let's look at the slow brain. This is our planner, our problem solver. This is our inner designer—the part of the brain that designs how we change our behaviors. It knows why and what we should do. It sets goals and focuses on executing the plan. In the case of Lisa, her slow brain was learning all kinds of new things about how, when, and what to eat. But she was loath to actually do what she learned because, in practice, her fast brain was running the show, always beating her slow brain to the cookie before it could do anything about it.

As you may expect, because we live mostly in autopilot mode, the slow brain is at a disadvantage when you design any new behavior because it takes more time to remember and activate the change. The slow brain is the tortoise in the fabled story *The Tortoise and the Hare*. It is the D'oh moment of Homer Simpson.

The slow brain has one advantage, however, which is to figure out how to level the playing field to its advantage—through *design*.

DESIGNING FOR FAST AND SLOW

If we wish to succeed in designing our behavior, we must account for the fast brain and the slow brain. If we do not design for both modes of thinking, we can end up like the after-school tutor in chapter 1 who had the most fabulously healthy year of her life only to completely stop all of those behaviors with no explanation as to how or why. In fact, whenever you go from being fabulously successful to *what happened?* or *why did I do that?*

you should be suspicious that there is a gap between your fast brain and your slow brain that you didn't see coming.

So how do we apply our knowledge of fast brain and slow brain? I find it easiest for designers I mentor if I give them a few rules of thumb they can use in their designs. Here are two top rules that I have seen work for everyone:

1. SLOW DOWN THE FAST BRAIN

I recently discussed designing behavior with a successful surgeon who wanted to improve her work-life balance. We spoke about how her booming career was wreaking havoc in her personal life. The qualities that made her successful in the workplace—being assertive, direct, and focused—worked against her at home with her family. Using fast brain–slow brain as a design model, we figured out that we had to slow down her fast brain's tendencies to snap at her family so she would have an opportunity to do something better. Psychological tools like cognitive behavior therapy (CBT) have been proven successful by interrupting the fast brain through substitute rules of thumb. For example, a famous CBT algorithm is counting to 10 when angry to exercise control over your temper. The surgeon and I designed a system wherein she would sit in her car for five minutes upon pulling into her garage. She would visualize taking off her surgeon mask, hat, and scrubs, and then putting on a robe as though she was on vacation. Then she pictured cleaning out her ears so she could listen. This worked for her, and she had better relations with her family. (But remember, her design is going to expire someday and she will need to redesign it.)

There are a couple design tricks to slow down the fast brain. As in the example of the surgeon, we can introduce a slow-brain activity to disrupt the automatic trouble caused by the fast brain. The fastest, most portable way to do this is by taking one slow, deep breath. Another method is introducing friction, or difficulty, like I did in my story of putting the cookies in the freezer to make it harder and slower to scarf them down. Finally, we can use triggers in our environment to snap us out of our fast-brain habits. I have heard of many useful examples such as putting a sticky note on the fridge that says "Does not contain emotional support," using stoplights as a reminder to take a deep breath, using a friend for accountability, and wearing a rubber band on the wrist and snapping it to disrupt negative thinking. Whatever it is that will get your attention and snap you out of your fast brain and into your slow brain is fair game!

2. SPEED UP THE SLOW BRAIN

The slow brain can compete with the fast brain if you can routinize the behavior. Because the fast brain works according to internalized algorithms (like, *if stressed, then eat comfort food*), your design can mimic an external algorithm to compete against it.

As an example, I had a friend who controlled his diet by eating the same three healthy meals every day: oatmeal in the morning, skinless chicken breast and broccoli for lunch, and a simple salad for dinner. He removed all decision-making, thinking, and emotion out of eating. He no longer had to use his slow brain to decide and no longer risked his fast brain making an impulsively unhealthy choice. Eventually, this initial slow-brain design became his fast-brain habit. He used routine and limiting choice to make healthy eating into a fast-brain default.

Before you object, let's admit that his strategy may not work for some people. It's an extreme example of how we can design for our own behavior and exploit our natural tendency to fast brain our way through life.

If variety is the spice of life for you, then your fast brain may rebel against chicken breast by the third day! Maybe a better design in that case would be to plan all meals on Sunday for the coming week—that way, you still get the variety while also preventing the fast brain from making unhealthy decisions on the fly.

Another way to give speed to the slow brain is to start with small steps and add on over time. My mentor Dr. Fogg created the Tiny Habits® program in this vein. When you start with a small behavior, it is easier to do, takes less time, and is lean enough to compete with the fast brain's set of habitual behaviors. The main goal is not to have to think about it—the new behavior should be as mindless as possible—again to mimic the fast brain's behaviors it is competing against. If you have to think every time about what you meant to do instead, then at some point your fast brain will get you. The cookie will be in your mouth before you remember your elaborate design of how you were going to stop yourself from eating cookies.

FAST-BRAIN SHORTCUTS

Heuristics are shortcuts that the fast brain uses to reduce our complex world to a manageable size so we can make sense of it. For our purposes, a heuristic can be defined as a mental shortcut that helps us reduce uncertainty and feel like we know what is going on. Heuristics are unconscious rules of thumb that help us quickly judge, take action, and move on. As you design to "catch" your fast brain and change its course, there are a few heuristics to know that will make your designing more effective.

The first major heuristic, grouping, is our fast brain's tendency to align like with like. It shortcuts by storing our experience in "this is like that" clusters. For example, whenever our brain is exposed to a new concept, the first thing it does is search for an existing analogy and link the two,[13] like banana and yellow. This happens in milliseconds. We create daisy chains of concepts, all reinforcing one another. And we are so convinced that our constructed reality is real that when our erroneous assumptions are pointed out to us, we often can't believe it.[14] A Harvard research project, Project Implicit, led by Mahzarin Banaji with Anthony Greenwald, used a timed test to expose the links of concepts in the unconscious minds of test subjects. These researchers demonstrated that there are groupings of unconscious biases that people have about race, mental health, and other topics.[15]

Grouping may get in your way as you design for new behaviors. If your fast brain has helped you feel knowledgeable by jumping to conclusions and grouping information together quickly, then it may be hard for you not to do this. If the behavior you wish to change involves not jumping to conclusions, the grouping heuristic poses an additional obstacle to design.

Priming is another type of heuristic that creates selective attention and memory. If, for instance, I ask you to look for everything that is red around you right now, I'm priming you with the color red. You have temporarily changed the filter through which you see the world. As a result, it has changed what you notice around you. You are biased to see red. Priming occurs when a trigger calls up other related things in our brain. It happens with either spoken language, visual cues, or simply sensations. For example, if you are holding a warm coffee cup in your hand as you're talking to somebody, you're going to feel warmly toward him or her. If you're holding a glass of ice water in your hand, you're going to feel a little bit distant and cold toward the person.[16] Likewise, if you sit on a hard chair while doing a difficult task, you experience the task as being harder than if you had been sitting on a soft chair. These relationships don't make logical sense, but to your unconscious mind, your fast brain, hard is hard, warm is warm, and cold is cold, regardless of form.

Priming and grouping can deceive us into thinking we are comfy cozy simply because our fast brain has reduced our sense of reality to something familiar. This might not always be for the best, however. A good friend of mine had an alcoholic father who was prone to fits of rage when he drank. After many years of healing herself, she was finding benefit in seeing a therapist to help her sort out her behavior patterns. One repeated pattern was her choice in men. She always dated bullies—like her dad. One day, upon describing yet another great guy she just met to her therapist, the therapist gave her words of wisdom:

"Given your history with a bullying father, it should be a big red flag when you first meet a man and it feels like you have known him forever. If you feel super familiar with him that quickly—RUN! It means you have replicated your father again."

We all have the tendency to fall into what is familiar because it feels like home. This is a heuristic. Even though it may be harmful for us, our fast brain gravitates toward what it knows from the past, rather than face the unknown. Recognizing this, we can design our way out of these defaults. We can expand our self-image to embrace change, a topic that we will explore in the next chapter.

Heuristics are the unconscious settings in the brain that color our ability to perceive things. Because they are unconscious, we don't notice them. We like to believe that we are completely aware of what's going on, that we see everything clearly and objectively, and that we're not just relying on some emotional sense, or some bias, or priming, or brain trick. But this is not the case—in fact, we are very biased. And the key to designing your life is to be aware of what's happening in the fast brain so we do not repeat the same mistakes indefinitely. A coach for top executives once told me that her most challenging task is helping her clients see what they were doing unconsciously and repeatedly so they could change their behaviors. "It's like showing the water to the fish," she said.

SLOW BRAIN STRENGTHS AND WEAKNESSES

Our slow brain is basically our conscious mind. Whereas the unconscious fast brain can handle millions of inputs per second, the conscious slow brain has a smaller working memory and must sustain attention in order to maintain control of our behavior. This means there are things the slow brain is good at, and other things—not so much.

Two slow-brain functions, willpower[17] and decision making, have been confirmed by research to be in limited daily supply. This means that when we wake up in the morning, we have a full tank of each, but then we start burning them down with each cookie we resist or each decision we make during the day. For example, you may have noticed that at the end of a long day of making decisions at work, you can hardly decide what to have for dinner. We can only exert so much willpower over temptations and make only so many decisions before we exhaust our stores. And when we run out of these slow-brain functions our fast brain takes over and shortcuts us through the rest of the day. We go on autopilot until we can replenish by morning.

Knowing this when you design means two things: (1) do not burn up your willpower on avoidable environmental triggers, and (2) don't put yourself at risk for making key decisions at the end of the day. In the first case, having a cake on your counter is a willpower challenge you will lose—it just takes time. Sure, you're fine most of the day and walk by the cake 20 times without cracking. But then the sun goes down, the kids go to bed, and POP goes the last burst of willpower you had—now your shields are down and the cake is coming in for a landing!

Likewise, make sure you do not have to make critical healthy decisions late in the day. As just mentioned, the classic mistake here is waiting too long to decide on what is for dinner. The closer you get to winging it on your way home from work, the more you risk going with the burger and fries combo offered up by your fast brain as a shortcut. Instead, you could "speed up" the slow brain to compete with the fast brain by preparing everything on Sunday so dinners are ready and healthy. Or, you could "slow down" and override the fast-brain default by planning out a healthy dinner earlier in the day while you still have decision-making power. When and how you design such behaviors makes all the difference.

The slow brain can also use design as an advantage over the fast brain to benefit us by committing ourselves at a future time. Neuroscientist Dr. David Eagleman uses the example of the Ulysses Contract, referring to a design that binds us in the future, as a way to follow our slow brain's plans while avoiding our fast brain's tendencies. It refers to the character Ulysses who had his crew tie him to his ship's mast so he could listen to the Sirens' song without helplessly jumping overboard to his death. Just like Ulysses, our slow brain can set a contract in motion that prevents our fast brain from acting on impulse and throwing us overboard.

PAST SELF, FUTURE SELF

Treating the past self and the future self like a relationship between two close friends has helped me design. This idea came from one of our team design meetings in my behavior design firm, engagedIN. We regularly explore and create new design concepts that help people change their behavior. At one particular creative session, I posed this question to my team: How good is your past self at getting your future self to change? In our discussion, we figured out that the future self could rebel, resent, get bored, or comply in response to the design (or Ulysses Contract) made by the past self (aka slow brain). We also discovered that successful behavior change always comes from iterations by the past self until it finds just the right "mouse trap" for the future self.

One of our designers had a super-healthy friendship between her past and future selves, even going so far as saying that if her future self did not follow the past self's design, she would feel like she was letting herself down. Another designer described how his future self does whatever it wants, spontaneously and regardless of what the past self had planned. His relationship between his past and future selves was a bit rebellious. For the rest of us, some had dysfunctional relationships between their past self and their future self; others had healthy, agreeable ones.

How about you? How good do you think your past self is today at designing for your future self to change behavior? Is your past self a tyrant, putting together harsh, inflexible schedules or making strict, large-scale changes? Does your future self rebel like a teenager or resent the design it has been given to follow? Or are your two selves in harmony, and do they cooperate, sharing trust and compassion between them? (By the way, the same questions apply if you are designing the behavior of someone else, like a family member, because in both cases you are managing a relationship between a designer and the one experiencing the design.) Either way, the quality of this relationship greatly impacts your success, so it is definitely worth asking what your future self would do in response to the design you're creating.

MYSTERY SOLVED

Back to our common experience of the gap of "I know what to do, I don't know why I don't do it." We can now understand it like this: We don't do what we should because our fast brain's habits and short cuts are beating out our slow brain's plans and intentions. But there is a solution! Our slow brain possesses the power of design as a way we can close this gap. To do this well, we must make sure that the designs created by our past self are pleasing and inspiring for our future self.

Fast Brain and Slow Brain Design

Here are some questions to design for the gap between the slow brain and the fast brain. Remember to mix in a healthy dose of empathy and compassion as you design.

What is it that you want to change?

_____

_____

What would your slow brain design to change it?

_____

_____

_____

What aspects of your fast brain (habits, quick judgments, shortcuts, associations) control your current behavior?

_____

_____

_____

_____

How might your slow-brain design lose out to your fast brain? Under what conditions?

_____

_____

_____

_____

_____

What design would slow down or hinder your fast brain and prevent it from dominating or sabotaging your slow brain's plan?

_____

_____

_____

What else can you do to strengthen your slow brain's chance of success? Remember, you can favor the slow brain by making the new behavior super-easy, automatic, or mindless like your fast brain, or favor your slow brain with memory triggers or social supports.

_____

_____

_____

_____

Notes

④

me, not me

All men should strive to learn before they die what
they are running from, and to, and why.

—James Thurber

first met Ms. Williams when I pushed past the stiff white curtain surrounding her gurney—the ER is not designed for privacy—and locked eyes with her frowning middle-aged daughters. Head elevated, the gray-haired, large-bodied Ms. Williams gasped for air from her oxygen mask, as her eyes flashed with a strong stare that said "don't mess with me." She was a fighter.

"Hello, Ms. Williams. My name is Kyra, and I am a medical student here to evaluate you..."

But I was quickly cut off.

"Where are the *real* doctors? Don't you see she can't breathe?! Go get someone who can help us!" The daughters were not interested in my help, and their mother seemed equally dissatisfied with my status. This was their first hospital experience. Rocky and tense, we began our journey together.

Ms. Williams had a nasty diagnosis: pericardial effusion. This meant she had fluid around her heart; it was most likely caused by a serious issue like cancer. Ms. Williams and her daughters spent their time complaining and fighting with the hospital staff. I couldn't blame them. Several mistakes had been made by the lab and by one of the residents, causing repeated tests and prolonged worry. Everything that could go wrong had gone wrong.

In the face of some life-threatening issues and as her hospital stay dragged on into weeks, Ms. Williams held her feisty attitude, especially against me as the most junior person on the team. However, I knew something she and her daughters didn't. They were going to get the most attention from me because the "real" doctors didn't have time for them. Attention to patients was the value I brought and the luxury I had as a medical student.

The days dragged forward. Numerous tests and blood draws and procedures were done trying to find the underlying cause of the fluid around Ms. Williams' heart. She had complication after complication, including a life-threatening pulmonary embolism. I saw her strength and fight yield into helplessness and despair with each needle stick, each morning round, each inconclusive test. She and her daughters started to ask me more questions and I would translate all the medical jargon into normal language for them.

One afternoon, after being on call all night, I dropped by her hospital room to find Ms. Williams alone. She vented to me how frustrated and hopeless she was getting. I must have been the bottom of the barrel of people she wanted to share that with.

"Well, what if you focus on something that makes you happy out there," my head motioned to the window, "in your normal life. What normally makes you happy?"

She perked up slightly. "The ocean. I love to walk my dog at the ocean every morning."

We talked about her happy memories of the ocean, her family and dog, then I left for the day.

On my way home, I was replaying the conversation and what it meant. *The ocean*, I thought; *her heart is the ocean*. OK, then... I will bring her the ocean!

Exhausted and numb, I arrived home, breastfed my four-month-old baby, and crashed next to my husband. I barely could wake to my 4:00 a.m. alarm. Morning rounds started at 6:00 a.m., so I had to move quickly. I put on my scrubs and a jacket, washed a near-empty mason jelly jar, and drove out to Ocean Beach on the other side of San Francisco.

In almost pure darkness, I navigated my way from the parking lot to the beach using the sounds of the waves crashing. It was windy and cold. No one else was around.

With somewhat ceremonial affect, I removed my shoes to connect with the cold sand and silently offered my respect and gratitude for Mother Ocean (hoping I wouldn't get "anointed" with a big wave). I slowly bent down and offered the little jar into the next foamy, sandy wave until it filled. Running back to my car, I felt fully awake and alive—a feeling that often was lost amidst my medical student life.

I arrived at the hospital by 5:00 a.m. and started pre-rounding on my patients. This involved waking each patient, doing a physical exam, and sometimes sticking them with needles to draw blood. This is not a pleasant way to wake up, especially when you're sick enough to be there in the first place.

I entered Ms. Williams' room, instinctively approaching it as if it were a sacred sanctuary, carrying my little jar of ocean as if it were holy water. As I self-consciously awoke her, Ms. Williams groggily flickered her eyes until they were open.

"I brought you the ocean, Ms. Williams," I said softly, placing the jar on her tray stand.

She smiled with wet eyes. "You didn't! Oh my goodness, I can't believe it! Yes, yes! The ocean is here!" Her smile stretched into its fullness, the first time I'd seen that level of radiance. "Thank you, thank you!"

My eyes teared up too. Words didn't come. I was completely *with* her.

From that day forward, Ms. Williams and I worked on her situation as a team—a team of equals. She returned to her previously powerful self, demanding answers from the doctors and making decisions for herself. She was assertive about getting her physical therapy and had her daughters bring in food when the hospital cuisine was not to her liking. She was able to go home early and conduct the rest of the tests as an outpatient— on her own terms.

Weeks later, I received a small package in my student mailbox. Ms. Williams had sent me a leather and silver bracelet with a tiny card that said, "Thank you for bringing my ocean back to me."

Holding the precious gift, I closed my eyes and whispered, "Thank *you*. For teaching me."

Ms. Williams' story reminds us of what we all want: to simply live as who we are. We each want to be at our "ocean," our Spirit connection. We want to express our gifts, talents, and even neuroses—and be loved for all of it. We want to be seen and heard and appreciated for the unique being that we are. We want to feel smart, capable, valuable, and—well, to feel like ourselves!

I have found many people in the healthcare field say things like "patients need to manage their health so they can live better." This usually means they want people to do what the system wants them to do, because the system thinks it knows what's best—according to the data. It is a well-meaning but blindly insensitive statement. That's not what we as humans want and it is not how we behave.

We don't manage our health. We manage our self-image.

In fact, everything we do or don't do can be explained by whether it serves our self-image. We spend most of our energy promoting the self-image we want to project, maintaining the self-image we have already built, or hiding the self-image we don't want others to see. Our self-image runs in the unconscious fast brain and serves as the chief operator of our behavior. All emotions, motivations, and fast-brain shortcuts are influenced or even dictated by our self-image.

ME, NOT ME

Where does the self-image, or sense of "me," sit in the brain? That is currently a tricky question, but scientists are honing in on the answer. Recent research has identified that consciousness, or awareness of self, does not arise from just one structure in the brain. Instead, it emerges from the coordinated activity of cells in a network of structures including the insula, anterior cingulate, and the medial prefrontal cortex.[18] Additionally, we have an area of our prefrontal cortex that appears to be our center for rumination. Rumination is a self-referencing loop, like *does he like me*, *how did I do*, and *is this shirt Me*. When the prefrontal cortex is not pondering such questions, it's busy judging us: *I did such a good job* or *I really screwed that up*. This brain area has been shown to be more active in people with anxiety and depression, the thought being that constantly ruminating about one's performance and status plays a part in these conditions.

Therefore, perhaps depression and anxiety are in part diseases of too much *Me* brain activity.

Regardless, it is safe to say that within microseconds the brain areas responsible for our self-image can form a reaction, positive or negative, to any new experience or information. Our brain is constantly consulting with our self-created identity, or self-image, to make sense of the world.[19] And this mostly happens unconsciously; our fast brain's self-image makes a quick judgment, *is this me or is this not me*, and either connects or moves on.

We have all experienced our me/not me filter at work. For example, the clothes you are wearing right now at one point or another passed the me/not me test for you to have chosen them. But they may fail the test after some passing of time—for example, when you no longer consider a particular jacket to be "you" because you have gained a few pounds or it is no longer in style and you have a self-image of being a stylish dresser.

When we encounter something new, we have an immediate fast-brain impression. We know right away if we want to dive in or if we want to walk (or run!) in the other direction. Think about how we surf channels, music, or websites. With little to no thought, we quickly opt out of things that are *Not Me* and hit the back button, the channel button on the TV remote, or the music app thumbs-down. We are even blind to anything the we consider *Not Me*, like when we look at a magazine rack and only see those we would read. Our fast brain is helping us filter out the "noise" in our world, and the self-image is its go-to filter.

L et's experience this me/not me concept for ourselves. (You will need to put the book down where you can read it while you do this.) I want you to hold your hands in front of your chest, palms facing each other, about chest-width apart. Spread your fingers wide open.

Now quickly slap your palms together and interlace your fingers, holding them in front of you. Keep holding and look down at your fingers. Which thumb is on top? Notice how your hands feel together. This is your *Me* center at work.

Now bring your hands back to the open position as before. You are going to do the same thing, but this time you will put your other thumb on top. Quickly—go! Hold your hands together like that. Now, how does this feel? Weird, right? Maybe a little uncomfortable? Do you want to put the other thumb back on top? This is your *Not Me* place. When you feel like you have had enough, you can unlace your fingers and keep reading.

You can see by doing this exercise how strongly we want to get back to the sense of *Me*, right? That's the self-image, aka our comfort zone, showing itself—showing us how it can generate a sensation strong enough to make us want to change our behavior back to our old ways. And that's just a little finger-interlacing exercise! Imagine if you actually design something life changing, like eating a paleo diet, becoming a triathlete, or stopping smoking? This is what we mean when by stepping outside our comfort zone; we have put the wrong thumb on top and our self-image, our *Me*, is freaking-the-hell out!

So, what does your *Me* sound like? Try this.

Go ahead and close your eyes for a full minute and simply notice how you talk to yourself.

Now do it again, but try to completely stop talking to yourself. (Don't feel bad, 99.99 percent of people can't.)

If you're doing this for the first time, you may be shocked by the nonstop, random chatter that you hear. This chatter is also more often negative than positive. (Remember, if some-one talked to us like we talk to ourselves, we would not be their friend!) These are our ruminations at full volume. This is the sound of our self-image.

ALL SUFFERING ARISES FROM SELF-IMAGE

When I first started meditating years ago, my teacher, Sylvia, in one of my first classes said something I have since always remembered, "All suffering arises from self-image." This means we spend tons of our time and energy either trying to promote our positive self-image or trying to avoid being seen as having a negative self-image. Both cause us suffering. If we don't look or act right 100 percent of the time, we suffer for not being able to promote our positive self-image. If we get misunderstood and others think we suck, we suffer for not being able to hide our negative self-image. We suffer because we lose control over promoting our good *Me* to others or hiding and covering up for our bad *Me*. All that brokering behavior—back and forth, back and forth—it's exhausting!

The algorithm for our self-image sits deep in the unconscious. And this makes it super-tricky to understand. There are probably thousands of unique self-image "scripts" that we run while interacting with our world. Our self-image is a many-layered equation of how we learned to guard against negative experiences while maximizing our time with positive experiences. Think about how the self-image you project changes when you are at work, at school, or at home. Behavioral psychologists call this code switching, which means that in response to any particular situation, we lead with a self-image tailored to succeed in that context.[20]

As behavior designers, the question we want to ask is which self-image will rise to the surface if I do X (X being a design to try out)? If we only knew what is encoded into our self-image and the hierarchy of how it presents itself, we could design ourselves to do anything! We could align with our positive self-image and avoid the defenses around our negative self-image.

Put another way, self-image is kind of like an operating system. It runs in the background all the time. Our behaviors are like programs that run on top of this operating system. All behaviors that we see in ourselves are sourced from some aspect of our self-image. What we currently do—our default behaviors—are compatible with the system. New behaviors are sometimes not. They are foreign, *Not Me* viruses that the system wants to remove. In this chapter and the next, we are dealing with how our behavior and our self-image coincide, and how new behaviors can become integrated into the *Me*.

Because it is like our hidden operating system, we sometimes don't see how our self-image filtering for me/not me blocks our efforts to change. I'm reminded of a dear person in my life that has always felt troubled by her weight. She's absolutely beautiful, but her perception of her weight has caused her a lot of suffering. Over the years, she has lost weight and regained it multiple times. It's a pattern that a lot of people go through, and, of course, the habenula, counting failures and lowering motivation, is no friend in the process.

Sitting with her and having that heartfelt conversation, I wanted to know more about her yo-yo weight experience. I asked her about her self-image and how it played into her behaviors.

"Well, I was always an overweight kid. I was always the one in school that was picked last in gym class—that sort of thing," she said. "We grew up in a rural small town and I received tons of praise for my baking. That felt really good, to take care of people and make them happy through baking for them. I suppose it became part of my identity."

"That's deep," I reflected, "So how did that affect your efforts to diet over the years?"

She went on putting together the puzzle. She described going on strict diets, vegetarian, Atkins, you name it. Each time she lost weight and felt great. But diets obviously don't involve a lot of baking. She found herself returning to the baking—and soon after, returning to her previous weight. Something in her dieting design was not working.

We connected the dots. She had a primary self-image as an overweight kid. She had another strong self-image as an amazing baker from which she derived a lot of pleasure and praise. She shared an insight: "When I go on a diet, I miss my baking more than anything. It's *Me*."

A couple years have passed now and she has been designing around this problem within her self-image. After a few more unsuccessful periods of no baking, she has embraced that she has to bake—something. So, designing for the amazing baker self-image, she has tinkered with her recipes and iterated on her design. She has started to bake only little things, like itty-bitty muffins. She also has used healthier sweeteners to replace some of the sugar and has experimented modifying her favorite recipes with whole grains and bran.

Another way to understand this is by understanding motivation. Each of her self-images, whether overweight kid or awesome baker, ignites a motivation for certain behaviors. No one motivation drives our behavior all the time; motivations are more impermanent than that. They are like ocean waves that roll in and roll out—strong ones canceling out weaker ones. Using this metaphor to understand her behavior, imagine that the drive to lose weight is like a small wave (maybe even a *Not Me*) compared to the tsunami-sized motivation wave of the amazing baker, who expresses and receives love through baked goods. The amazing baker tsunami overwhelms the dieter surface wave, and—voilà!—freshly baked bread.

When we start to think of these competing aspects of our self-image and the waves of motivations that they throw off, it becomes obvious that our self-image is very dynamic. Therefore, if we intend to change our behavior, and at first it does not succeed, that does not mean that we are weak, undisciplined, or unmotivated. We are simply experiencing the competing waves of stronger, self-image-based motivations that are overwhelming the motivation for doing that new behavior.

Similarly, just as the ocean has both surface waves and powerful, enormous deep ocean undercurrents that are not visible, so too our motivations can show up as shallow and ephemeral or deep and enduring. Remember from chapter 1 that every design we create to change our behavior has an expiration date. This is because these designs ride on the waves of our motivation, which source from the deep water of our self-image. If the design works with our self-image or becomes compatible with our self-image over time, then it becomes a habit, a part of the deep ocean of the *Me*. The expiration date gets extended.

One of my most direct conversations on behavior change and self-image happened unexpectedly at a cocktail party at the Harvard Connected Health Symposium after my keynote speech. As often happens to me when I talk about behavior change with people, others share their experiences. Mark, a top executive at a large healthcare company, shared his own experience of trying to change his behavior. Holding his glass of red wine up near his face so I could see both simultaneously, he told me the following story:

"You see, my vice is—I love wine," he glanced lovingly at the glass in his hand. "I've been studying and collecting boutique and rare wines for years, even built a wine cellar in my basement to hold it all," he said as he took another sip. "But here's the thing, lately wine has given me a gut. At my peak, I had gained like 40 extra pounds! I mean, I'm not that guy! I can't be that guy! I was the guy with the six-pack in high school!"

"And it's all because my knees are shot. I used to just play hoops or ski and didn't gain a pound. But after four surgeries on each, my doc says my basketball and mogul skiing days are over."

"Oh wow, so now what do you do for exercise?" I asked.

"Well, I tried to play basketball still; I've always been an athlete so team sports motivate me. Plus, it's a male bonding thing. But after one pick-up game my knees hurt so bad I literally could not walk. So I hit the gym. I tried. But I was totally bored—couldn't get myself to do anything."

"Then what?" I tracked.

"I hired a trainer. Not just any trainer, but a real ball buster! I picked him because of that. I needed someone who would get in my face and scream 'C'mon, you lazy ass!' He makes me work harder than I ever would alone. I've lost 20 pounds already."

The thought of someone yelling at me during a workout made me cringe, so I wanted to know why this worked for him. I asked whether he had ever been yelled at during exercise.

His eyes searched inquisitively upward to the right, "Yeah, my high school football coach screamed at us during workouts. I loved it. And I would push myself harder and harder," he recalled.

Do you see the motivations battling for control in Mark's self-image? Let's count them up. The self-images of basketball team player and mogul skier have retired like athletes after career-ending injuries. Since their retirement, the wine collector self-image has been winning over the six-pack high school football player in most cases and has caused a 40-pound belly fat problem. But now the high school football player has been making a comeback and has hired a personal trainer to try to undo the damage that the wine collector has done.

And this is exactly what I described to Mark. He swirled his wine glass, head nodding, smirking as he took it in.

"Wow, I never looked at it that way, but that makes total sense! I mean I lost 20 of the 40 pounds that I gained from drinking wine, but I think I'm going to have to choose between that inner six-pack (abs) athlete or my inner wine lover," he reflected.

This happens to all of us: various self-images take turns running our behavior. One day we are buying a fine wine at an auction, the next we are hiring a personal trainer who reminds us of the old coach. And both are *Me*.

And that's why we need to design around the self-image—every aspect of it.

DESIGNING *WITH* THE SELF-IMAGE

Mark's story shows us that whenever we design something in our life, it must work with our self-image for it
to stick. For Mark, the regular gym experience did not
connect with any part of his self-image, so it died quickly.
It was not until he designed a workout that resonated
with his old high school self-image that he found success.
Yet he also had built up a more recent self-image around
collecting wine that was fighting with his inner high
school six-pack-abs athlete over the last 20 pounds of his
wine gut. Once he heard what was underlying his behavior—the struggle between these two characters—he was
in a position to design for what was really going on.

Without the knowledge of self-image battles, Mark's
efforts were doomed to fail. When his inner football
player could not work out hard enough to undo the
behaviors of the wine expert, he likely would have
blamed himself for his laziness in workouts or lack of
self-control for continuing to drink wine. He would have
fallen into the most common trap of all good people
who try to change their behavior without knowledge of
self-image: self-judgment.

To use self-image in your behavior designs, you do
not have to go through years of therapy and analyze

your unconscious and childhood memories. Just remember this: there are a few specific designs that will work with your self-image, but most others will not. As you iterate on behavior designs, the designs that do not work at all are outside of your *Me* center. Those that work for a short while are a little closer. Those that work a long time are spot on! You are like Goldilocks, trying the find the design that is "just right" for your self-image.

I often see well-meaning people who have figured out what works for them try to share it enthusiastically with others, either word-of-mouth or online. These are testimonials from evangelists. And, yeah, that will work with the self-image of some of the people who are exposed to that particular design, whether it be a meal plan or an exercise plan. But for the rest, it doesn't, and the habenula logs a failure. This is why it is critical to maintain the attitude of a designer—it is great to try the winning recipes of others as long as you never forget that you are only trying out a new design, somewhat like trying on an outfit in the store. We have all tried on something that seemed great on the rack but looked absolutely hideous once we put it on. When that happens, we put it back on the rack and keep shopping.

Putting it back and continuing to shop makes you a designer—the ability to move on, unscathed by failed attempts.

That is what I want you to do with the design suggestions and advice of others—stay in your power as a designer, and you and only you decide whether their recipe works for you. It is wonderful to be inspired by others, but you decide whether it fits in your *Me* center. Of course, there are thousands of ads, infomercials, and multibillion-dollar diet companies, celebrity trainers, financial advisors, and relationship experts all trying to convince you that if you just do what they do, you'll be fabulous. Not so. In my book (yes, this book), the best approach is to figure out what works with your self-image, then design and iterate until something sticks.

To me, it is as if you were a zookeeper. You wouldn't feed the same thing to every animal in the zoo, right? Likewise, the same advice or product or method cannot possibly work for every person in a population. People are unique, and their self-image is equally unique to them. Instead, I see it something like this: Weight Watchers works really well for *X* percent of the population, CrossFit for *Y* percent, Yoga for *Z* percent. Each of these solutions has its place, and each of them docks into the self-images of their followers, like a behavioral lock and key.

Here's what I mean.

As a child, I was encouraged—almost defined—by my relatives always saying, "Oh, that Kyra, she can eat so much and not gain a single pound!" That made its way into my *Me* center. Skinny as a stick, I would eat seconds, even thirds, for dinner. I would snack on whatever I wanted, whenever I wanted. (*Sniff, those were the days!) Of course, the day came when I hit puberty and I did gain a pound, then 5 pounds, then 20. My "I can eat whatever I want" self-image had run into a snag.

So I tried the conventional advice at the time: a low-fat diet. That totally did not work because fat is what helps you register as full, and I never felt full. I also tried the six small meals advice because it was supposed to help stabilize your blood sugar and, therefore, stabilize your hunger. But I ended up eating more because I never felt like I ate a real meal. I didn't know what was going on and why I was unable to succeed in my efforts. Finally, I figured it out. My self-image was not connecting with any of these eating plans. I put two and two together and realized that as a person who thought she could eat whatever she wanted, the most important sensation for me to feel like *Me* was volume! Total epiphany! My *Me* had to feel the slight stretch of my stomach to (unconsciously) register that I was myself and had eaten enough. When I started eating for volume with healthy foods like apples and nuts, I got a grip on my eating and better controlled my weight.

As part of my work as a designer of behavior change, I have asked thousands of people about their food, exercise, and health habits. As a public health professional, I have studied health data patterns for tens of millions. From this, what I know is that what people stick to and what works for them always has a heuristic link to their self-image. Remember that a heuristic is an unconscious shortcut that the brain uses as a rule of thumb to save us time and help us feel like we know what's going on. In the case of people's behaviors, whether eating, exercising, saving money, or relating with others, I have seen time and time again that a heuristic will either make or break a person's attempt to change their behavior. And if that one heuristic, that one important rule of thumb, is missing from their design, they will quit that behavior.

Here are a few examples of people I have run into that illustrate this observation:

- a smoker who always needs to have something in his mouth gains weight when he quits because he fulfills that heuristic with food

- a competitive athlete who cannot get herself to exercise without a deadline like a race or a season because she has a heuristic around extreme training to compete

- a woman who cannot take time out for herself because her heuristic of being a good mom means she has to feel the burn of self-sacrifice for her children

- a Southern man who cannot stick with a low-fat diet because he has a heuristic requiring crunchy fried food at every meal

In each of these cases, there is a core sensation that is somehow connected with the person's sense of *Me*.

I'll take that one step further. I have seen this so consistently that I am convinced that people fall into heuristic types based on their self-image. For example, there are unique eater types, exercise types, and money management types, all defined by the heuristics that run in their brains. For example, Mark in our story is a team exerciser type. Watching my own behavior, I type myself as a volume eater because eating a big meal is *Me*. My sister, on the other hand, absolutely must put some type of sauce on her food and cannot eat anything dry. Therefore, a healthy eating plan for her would have to be designed with her wet-food type in mind. Yet others are deprivation eaters, whereby going too long without food invokes various degrees of *Not Me* panic. Still others are meat-eater types. For example, when working with inner city youth, I noticed that they do not think it is a meal unless they have meat on their plates. This makes sense given the financial struggles in their childhood and meat being scarce when times were tough. The heuristic of eating meat means *Me*, abundant and safe, and the absence of animal protein means *Not Me*, loss and uncertainty.

But who designs for this kind of thing? What program have you seen that approaches it in this way? None to my knowledge. I think what is going on is that a particular organization with a particular approach (like Weight Watchers, CrossFit, Alcoholics Anonymous) finds and retains those with self-images and heuristics that are compatible with that approach. One size fits some. Everyone else falls through like a sieve. It is like the zookeeper who feeds all the animals hay, and only those who thrive on that type of food survive.

As a designer of your life, it is up to you to be the proverbial matchmaker between you and what works for your *Me*. And knowing something, anything, about your self-image—even simply asking yourself what comprises your self-image—goes a long way toward your success. Even if you join an organization that uses a particular approach, you can be more effective at picking the right one and not wasting time on a bunch that will trigger your sense of *Not Me*.

WHEN SELF-IMAGE FAILS US

We can usually count on our self-image to seek pleasure and avoid pain, to filter for me/not me, and to promote a positive image and hide a negative image. There are a few exceptions to this rule. First, in cases where unhealthy experiences or beliefs have made it into our *Me* center, our self-image can work to our detriment. Examples include staying in abusive relationships because our parents conditioned us to feel that this is normal—our *Not Me* alarms do not go off, rather our unconscious *Me* algorithm is abuse equals normal. Similarly, in areas of low self-esteem, the *Me* may be surrounded by toxic people who put us down, but we don't fight back because it resonates with our low sense of self. It is the same principle: in the *Me* center of our brain lies what we feel is our dominant thumb on top or our awkward other thumb on top. If the *Me* thumb is on top, we ignore it—we are "home"—even if home is not so healthy.

Another example of where our self-image can be misleading comes from the field of consumer marketing. This field specializes in selling us anything and everything it can. Billions of dollars are spent to understand the human psyche and what will lead to purchases. Therefore, in many ways this field has contributed key insights into human behavior. One such insight is the difference between actual self-image and aspirational, or idealized, self-image.

It turns out that just as self-image drives most of our habitual behavior, it also provides the heuristics of how we decide on what we purchase and what we don't. In the case of actual self-image, a purchase is straightforward. For instance, a person who is a marathon runner goes out and buys a marathon-specific training watch that records their times and improves their performance. Marathon self-image, marathon product. In the case of aspirational self-image purchases, however, people buy things based on who they want to be. In this case, a non-runner buys a marathon watch because they like the image and maybe hope to do that someday.

Not surprisingly, products we buy that are closer to our actual self-image get used far more than those we buy for our aspirational self-image. In fact, the things that we buy that are not in alignment with our actual self-image, or fall out of alignment with it, make up 100 percent of the clutter we own. Prove it. Look around your house. How about over there in the corner? Remember that top-of-the-line home treadmill you bought last January only to watch it morph into the most expensive laundry hanger ever? How about those books you hoard that you swear you will read someday? Did your aspirational self-image of an imagined tomorrow buy those skinny jeans with the tag on them still, that you knew you would fit into in no time? Some would say that buying aspirational things motivate them—but as we will see in the next chapter, that is an unstable, fleeting motivation and rarely works.

The last way our self-image works against us is through the anchoring effect it has on our behavior. Imagine that your *Me* center has a bungee cord attached to it. This means that whenever you change your behavior, the bungee cord is stretched away from the comfort zone of *Me*. When we buy aspirational products or otherwise set ourselves up for massive changes ("I'm going to run 10 miles a day, starting at dawn tomorrow!"), we stretch this bungee far outside our comfort zone. And it can last. For a while. But at some point the *Me* center alarms, "hey, wait a minute, *Me* is not like this, *Me* is like that," and it abruptly snaps us back into our old comfy behaviors. Our inner fat kid exclaims, "hey, wait, this skinny body doesn't feel like *Me*." The alcoholic objects, "sobriety feels weird." The codependent says, "hey, wait, no one needs me anymore." The other thumb is struggling to stay on top. We went too far too fast and— snap—we relapse.

The difficulty in assimilating extreme change into the self-image is why gastric bypass surgery has such a high rate of long-term failure. The unconscious mind of such patients has been programmed over years that *Me* equals high volumes of food. But then after surgery, the unconscious is like, "whoa, wait a minute, *Me* doesn't eat tiny meals!" And even when overeating causes pain and vomiting for these patients due to their new tiny stomach, the self-image fights to get back to the old comforts of *Me*—even so far that those with adjustable bands end up stretching their tiny stomach back out. It is not rational; it's self-image.

Another surprising experience reported by people who are addicted to heroin further illustrates this phenomenon. My conversations with people in recovery totally reversed my judgment that they do drugs to get the dopamine release and feel high. One young man completely changed my mind when he told me in a matter-of-fact tone, "I don't do heroin to get high. I do heroin to feel normal." What is that but self-image? That's code for *Me*. Heroin had made its way into his *Me* center.

AGAIN, WITH THE COMPASSION

We go back to compassion. Always back to compassion. It is imperative that we hold ourselves with compassion while we examine the fact that everything we create—what we do and say, what we buy, who we relate to—is rooted in our self-image. And when we change our behavior, it creates disruption to our self-image. And when we disrupt ourselves, we feel groundless and uncomfortable. When we are groundless and uncomfortable, we can resort to self-defenses and relapse to old behavior.

I teach my students that it is as if we have a *Me* immune system. Now, of course, this is just a metaphor; there is no second immune system in the body. But my point is that our new behaviors fall under attack by our sense of *Me*, just like bacteria or toxins that enter the body are attacked by white blood cells. Those cells recognize when something is foreign—when something is *Not Me*.

Things that newborn babies are exposed to, like gut bacteria, get tolerated as part of their self. They are not constantly fighting against everything that they're exposed to; things are allowed in.[21,22] As they get older and they encounter viruses or bacteria, then their immune system recognizes, "That's not me. I have to fight it."

Similarly, whatever behaviors we were "bathed in" as a child—whether it's praise or abuse—counted as self, as *Me*, and we will not fight against them. We think those behaviors are us. On the contrary, new and foreign behaviors are *Not Me* and get attacked—especially behavior changes that are too quick and dramatic.

So what does all of this mean for designing your life?

First and most importantly, it means that you have to change gradually so you don't stretch the bungee so far that you get a snapback. If you go slowly, then the new behavior will slowly feel like *Me*. Don't trip the wire. Don't poke the *Not Me* bear. Baby steps help you tiptoe through the field and not set off a trip wire of *Not Me*. Self-image has to adjust in step with behavior changes. Otherwise, the changes may not be sustainable.

My suggestion here is that in areas where you want to design for change, your success rate will go way up if you take the time to examine how the various aspects of your self-image may be operating in the background. We know from the finger-interlacing exercise that self-image can create a strong pull toward an old behavior. It can trip you up, and your behavior can shift back to old habits way in advance of your slow conscious mind catching the shift. Therefore, examining what sits in your self-image *Me* center saves you a lot of time and heartache when you design for change.

As I shared earlier, I spent years of frustration and shame not knowing why I overate, but once I realized

I have a self-image of being a volume eater, I was able to design to work with that. I created a list of foods I could eat endlessly, thereby meeting my heuristic need to stretch my stomach. I also pay attention that once per day I have a stomach-stretching meal. No more deprivation, no more self-hatred.

Finally, you are your own designer. Whatever you find out there in the world, a system, a guru, a community that helps you—great! But never ever give up your God-given power to design for who you are. Behavior design involves the endless practice of learning who you are, what works for you now, and when that inevitably changes, tinkering with a new way to engage. If you've tried to lose weight, change your spending habits, or make other big changes in the past and those changes didn't stick, start again with the powerful knowledge to follow what is inside of you—your original instructions. Be compatible with your own operating system. Listen to yourself. Actually take the time to get to know her or him. Every great designer starts with empathy for their client. Remember that your self-image is the real client, and your slow brain is the designer.

Designing for My Me

How do you define *Me* and *Not Me*? What is this *Me* operating system that you're running? What are some *Not Me* things that you know you resist? Here's a slow-brain exercise for you to write down some helpful insights about your self-image.

What I want you to do is answer the following two questions until you completely run out of ideas. Go deeper and deeper until you literally go blank.

1. Complete this sentence as fast and as many times as you can:

I am a

_____

_____

_____

_____

_____

_____

_____

2. Complete this sentence as fast and as many times as you can:

I am not a

_____

_____

_____

_____

_____

_____

Review what you just wrote. Now, circle your top three answers for each question. Your first set of answers are *Me*, your second set are *Not Me*.

Anything surprise you? Any self-images seem more dominant or mature than others? These are the scripts you are running, and I bet you can match each of your behaviors to one or more of them.

To take this farther, do some journaling, with your top three self-images for *Me* and your top three for *Not Me* in mind. Here are some questions to help guide your insights:

When has this self-image helped me improve my life or design a better life for myself?

_____

_____

_____

When has this identity gotten in my way or
sabotaged me?

What needs to happen to stop that?

_____

_____

_____

_____

_____

_____

Now, placing your hand on your heart, take
three slow breaths to end this exercise. I also
suggest taking a moment to congratulate yourself and thank yourself for taking the time to
do this.

Trust that whatever you learned from this
exercise will stay with you, and that you will
start to notice it more and more.

Notes

⑤

finally, the truth about motivation

I used to think I was indecisive,
but now I'm not so sure.

—*unknown*

Elliot (not his real name), a middle-aged professional, went to see neuroscientist Antonio Damasio due to increasingly negative changes in his life. Several years prior, Elliot had undergone surgery to remove a benign brain tumor in the central part of his frontal lobe. He was physically fine and fully recovered from the surgery, cancer-free. Thankfully, he was able to return to his job, family, and life—or so it had seemed at first. But things got worse from there. His personal and even professional relationships fell apart. He lost his job, many friends, and divorced twice. None of his doctors knew why. After consulting with Dr. Damasio, a clear picture emerged of what had happened to Elliot.

During brain surgery to remove his tumor, Elliot had sustained damage to a structure called the amygdala. While his cognitive abilities—receiving sensations, working with numbers, weighing pros and cons—were not impaired in any way, he struggled terribly to make decisions. In an effort to help, Damasio studied Elliot's difficulty with making decisions, even simple ones, like picking a restaurant.

When asked which restaurant he wanted to go to, Elliot would start to weigh his options. One minute he would favor the food and service of one restaurant then switch to the location and pricing of the other. Listening to him, he sounded logical and smart. And he also was not lacking in motivation; he was plenty hungry. But he was trying so hard to reason it out, that the more he used his logic, the farther he seemed to be from his goal.

Unfortunately, this type of lengthy deliberation was a part of his daily life. And it was not just over restaurant choice. Elliot did this for every decision he had to make. Damasio told of a time when he had to finally interrupt

Elliot's lengthy monologue, set off in response to the simplest question:

"For our next appointment, would you prefer to come in on Tuesday or Wednesday?"

"Well, Tuesday would work well because... but Wednesday is also good because... but then again, Tuesday might be best if..."

So, how did a damaged amygdala wreak such havoc on Elliot's life?

The amygdala is nestled deep within the temporal lobe of the brain, the lower area of the cerebral cortex that lies between your temples and your ears. This strange-sounding name comes from the Latin meaning "almond," and the amygdala is indeed about the size and shape of an almond. There is an amygdala in both the right and left hemispheres of your brain. The amygdala's primary job is to judge incoming information and then report it to the rest of the brain such as *this is good; we want more of this* or *this is stressful and icky; run the other way!*—or anywhere in between.

The amygdala assigns emotions and meaning—the juice of life. It's how we can give a crap. Emotion gives a lift to decision making by enabling us to mark things as good, bad, or indifferent. Right or wrong, and we are often terribly wrong, we use emotion to feel like we know what the right decision is.[23] From there, our sensation is stored as emotional intensity that helps us take action (approach or avoid) more quickly.

But, what if we do not feel anything, like Elliot? Living with a damaged amygdala, our experiences would no longer be colored by emotion; everything would be shades of gray, making it nearly impossible to make choices. Without emotion, all information is flat. Option A and option B *feel* the same.

So how does emotion sway us? In short, it taps into our memories of past experiences. We are swayed by our historical data, that is, how a past experience made us feel.[24, 25] Let me say that again. When we make a decision, we base it on a memory of how we felt during a similar experience in our past, not on our current situation.

If you have ever watched a good friend make the same bad dating decisions over and over again, you have watched this emotional bias in action. And if you could see yourself from the outside, you would see that you also do this. The power of emotion to color our experience reminds me of a quote by Maya Angelou: "I've learned that people will forget what you said, people will forget what you did, but people will never forget how you made them feel."

Our emotional unconscious is so sticky, in fact, that it can gel several memories together.[26] If you have ever smelled a food that reminded you of your grandmother's cooking, you know what I am saying here. Your sense of smell, the olfactory center of the brain, sits right next to your main emotional circuitry. Good smells and pleasant emotions are often grouped together by the brain.[27] Hello, Grandma's cookies + warm fuzzy feelings!

DYNAMIC EMOTION

By and large, science traditionally hasn't been interested in focusing on subjective experiences like emotions, but neuroscientist Jaak Panksepp luckily didn't get that memo. He has been mapping out motivations and how they relate to the architecture and chemistry of animal brains—across many species—for about five decades now. He is a pioneer in a field that he named: affective neuroscience (which really just means emotion and brain).

Dr. Panksepp has demonstrated seven basic emotional neural networks that originate from deep brain structures (those in the hind, or primitive, brain) in animals. There are three negative emotions: rage, fear, and grief (i.e., from abandonment). There are three positive emotions: joy (play), caring (nurturing), and the sex drive. Finally, there is a dominant positive emotion—seeking—that Panksepp says trumps all. Seeking is the drive to forage for life's essentials: food, water, mate, and so forth. These emotion systems are labeled as positive or negative based on an animal's behavioral preference as indicated by a tiny electrode implanted in its brain that is stimulated by the animal's emotion. In other words, the animals enjoy and seek out positive emotion and try to avoid or escape negative emotion.

Among other things, Panksepp has demonstrated that rats laugh when tickled (for which he's been called the rat tickler) and that chickens and guinea pigs experience sadness in ways that are almost identical to humans, in terms of both subjective experience (as best we can tell) as well as brain anatomy and function. He also has shown that the physiology of motherhood is the same as the physiology of love.[28] These are colorful findings, and they point to valuable conclusions for us human animals. Simply put, the research shows that we all have emotions because they help us figure out what makes our survival more or less likely. Emotions are "ancestral tools for living."[29] Without them, like Elliot's personal relationships falling apart, we can lose the safety and support from our tribe. Without its herd, an individual animal's survival rate goes way down—and humans are social animals.

So, now you can see the power that emotions have in driving decisions and behavior, even survival. But, you might ask, what about motivation? What does motivation have to do with what I do or do not choose?

EMOTION VS. MOTIVATION

Warning. I am now going to shift how you think about motivation—because it is likely hurting you, or at least not helping you be more successful. We are going to ground our understanding of motivation in how it operates in the brain. We are going to look at it objectively, scientifically, so we can free ourselves from the emotional baggage it has accumulated through decades of pop psychology.

The most common misconception people have about behavior change is that they need more motivation. I hear it all the time: "I just need to get more motivated" or "I'm just not motivated enough." The assumption most people make is that if they can just pump up the motivation, the rest will take care of itself. Not so.

Motivation is an elusive term, used inaccurately much of the time. Even its dictionary definition is confusing, as we can see from www.dictionary.reference.com: "the state or condition of being motivated or having a strong reason to act or accomplish something." Huh?

I think an easier definition to remember is that motivation is the drive to do something. But having drive does not always lead to taking action. It reminds me of the definition of potential energy in physics: the energy something has because of its position within a system, such as a ball sitting at the top of a ramp that has yet to roll down. Motivation inside of us is like that ball, sitting at the precipice, increasing the potential that we may get moving.

Everyone has had the experience of feeling highly motivated to do something, only to forget or get distracted. Remember Lisa, the woman in my metabolic study who knew what to do but didn't know why she didn't do it? She was highly motivated to lose weight and eat healthy. Yet she was perplexed, even disappointed in herself, when her strong drive to do what she should do failed her. Motivation did not change her behavior—at least not entirely. There's another part to the mystery.

Why am I nitpicking over this concept? You may be saying to yourself, *OK, already; the word* motivation *is used inaccurately—so what?* Let me just say that I am the last person to dissect the meaning of words. To the contrary, I can be supercolloquial. But what I see when people like Lisa misunderstand motivation is that they beat themselves up for not having enough motivation— and every one of us is like Lisa at some point. Therefore, if you are going to iterate and design your life, let's make sure you have the truth about motivation.

When people say things like "I need to get moti-vated," what I think they really are saying is "I want to feel stronger about doing this, and I hope that will get me to do it." They are saying *motivation*, but really, they are talking about emotion. I believe people instinctively know that feeling stronger helps them decide, commit, and take action. That's why they pump themselves up emotionally—like athletes with headphones blasting pump-up tunes before a big game. If motivation is the ball at the top of the ramp, emotion is the finger that taps it over the tipping point. To illustrate how this works, let's look at an example of how motivation and emotion act in concert to change behavior.

Fitness events for charity, like Team in Training, are all the rage now. Using a behavior design eye, and your newfound knowledge of motivation and emotion, you now can figure out why these work. These pop-ular events stimulate both emotion and motivation in their participants to get them to do something that they would have trouble doing alone. First, the emotion is elevated through doing the activity with others; by putting people on teams there is mutual accountability and emotional support. Emotion is also amplified by the cause itself: breast cancer, Alzheimer's, AIDS—all very emotional issues. For example, you would never see a charity marathon that fights chapped lips. The cause is too wimpy. The emotions of suffering chapped lips would not match the intensity of training for a mara-thon. Finally, these events also tap into people's motiva-tion, or potential energy. By linking their drive to run a marathon to a bigger social cause, these events up the ante on motivation. Adding personal and social moti-vations together make it far more likely that the person will follow through. To further stabilize that motivation, the team interactions can provide social norms (e.g., we all go running together on Saturday morning) and com-munications that constantly remind each team member of their motivation.

Not only is *motivation* a murky definition as a word, but that is also how it shows up in our brain. It turns out that the neuroscience of what we call motivation involves a number of different areas in the brain, depending on the type and timing of motivation. In other words, there is not one "motivation center" in the brain where motivation lives. Rather, what scientists find is a litany of reward centers, our old friend the habenula, the amygdala, and other brain areas that activate in different combinations, all under the umbrella of what we call motivation. To further complicate things, studies have shown that there are many subtypes of motivations: intrinsic, extrinsic, goal-directed, anticipatory, gain and loss, to name a few. So, if the neuroscience is this complex, you can see why saying "I just need to get more motivated" is too abstract and amorphous to design a solution around.

Two types of motivation are more concrete for designing behavior: intrinsic and extrinsic. Intrinsic motivation in neuroscience refers to the stuff we do because we find it inherently rewarding. No one has to coax or praise us—we love to do it all by ourselves. The rewarding feelings associated with intrinsic motivation have been linked to the anterior insular cortex, an area of the brain where we feel autonomy, as well as the ventral striatum, an area where we process rewards. Putting two and two together, this means we feel independent, even empowered, when we are intrinsically motivated—and that feels rewarding.

Extrinsic motivation, by contrast, refers to the external reward or incentive received in exchange for doing something. A paycheck taps our extrinsic motivation. So does paying your kids for their good grades in school. In behavioral neuroscience, extrinsic motivation is a type of learning called Pavlovian-instrumental transfer (PIT), which is a super-complicated way of saying that rewarding someone to perform a task (instrumental conditioning) makes that reward twice as powerful for them. For example, corporate bonuses can become addictive as a reward for certain normative behaviors because of PIT. But there is also a price we must pay. In the brain, extrinsic motivation can map to the posterior cingulate cortex and angular gyrus, areas where we feel a loss of agency and control. Therefore, when we are rewarded externally, it triggers a form of motivation that makes us feel rewarded, but we do not feel that we control the reward—someone else does. It disempowers us.

Let's look at an example, one that is all too familiar. I once worked on a project that asked people about their biggest obstacle to exercising. Far and away the most common answer was not having the time. At the same time, almost everyone claimed they were motivated to work out more often than their fitness habits demonstrated. While it's true that life is busy and schedules can get hectic, that's just the surface story and not the truth about their motivation.

What is happening at a deeper level is that we may be derailed by an emotion that diverts us from our motivation to go to the gym. For instance, we may feel guilty for selfishly taking time for ourselves, or we may feel stressed at the thought of leaving our work behind, or feel bad about not finishing that project.

So is the issue really that people don't have time?

If you take all the emotion out and just stick with logic, every person has the same amount of time. Even people with extremely busy schedules have periods where they waste time: playing on their smartphone, watching TV, surfing the Internet, etc. Instead of the many distractions of the day, they could certainly fit in a high-intensity 10-minute workout, right? But instead of going to work out, people may choose to be with their kids. This may be fueled in part by the guilt people feel over not spending enough time with their family. What they say on the survey is that they don't have time, but their actions say that they feel guilty about doing something for themselves, so they neglect their own needs. That isn't a time issue—it's an emotional one.

Emotion powers motivation. Motivation catalyzes emotion. They work in sync. In the brain, they often co-arise, co-stimulate—sometimes like a chicken-and-egg loop. The intensity of emotion sparks the potential for the motivation. Stable motivation, fed by positive emotional memory over time, forms a positive feedback loop that strengthens that motivation further.

Remember chapter 3 talked about how there is a limited daily supply of decisions we can make? So, if emotion fuels our decisions and we have a finite number of decisions each day, that means that our most emotionally charged decisions will dominate and get our attention. As you are designing your life, you absolutely must pay attention to how much emotion you burn through. How wisely are you "spending" it? For instance, if your morning routine is to spend an hour hating your body and burning frustration just to pick what you are wearing that day, you must ask yourself, "is that how I want to spend my decision power today?" Steve Jobs always wore black turtlenecks and jeans. Always a designer, Steve purposely had a closet full of black turtlenecks and jeans. These uniform outfits strategically reduced his decision load every day. He conserved his emotions and decision making to pick designs and products that made billions of dollars. The more we burn through little, relatively unimportant decisions, the less energy we have for the critical decisions that make us more impactful designers.

In another example, every parent I have ever interviewed has noticed that when they are frazzled and it is the end of the day, they more easily give in to their kids' demands. Teens seem to be particularly good at exploiting this weakness—timing their badgering for post-dinner Fridays, when parents are cooked from a busy week and in a food coma! You normally would have high motivation to say no to the late curfew, yet in that instant, being low on decision-making power and perhaps drained of emotion, you give in. We all do. In our weary state, we would rather choose emotional equilibrium and recovery than take on an emotional debate with a teen—especially since, in that moment, that teen has 100 percent of their focus on negotiating a later curfew!

What I am pointing out is that none of this is static. We are different in the morning than in the evening. We get distracted. We think it's a time issue when really it's emotional discomfort that shapes our priorities. We think we need more motivation when we are really referring to emotion. Meanwhile, our brain is sparking with emotional and motivational circuitry in all kinds of combinations. All this points to the moving, dynamic, and temporal nature of emotion and motivation—and how our current way of thinking about them doesn't help us design a better way.

A DESIGN METAPHOR FOR MOTIVATION AND EMOTION

It is easy and helpful to think of motivation like it is a wired light bulb. It can shine constant and bright. It may also be faulty, flickering on and off, or even be totally burned out. A light bulb can be outshined by a stronger light bulb and can overpower light bulbs weaker than itself. Motivation can be a stable and strong light, or it can be flickering and weak. One motivation can dominate, or outshine, another temporarily or always. The light bulb's wiring can be stable and robust. Alternatively, it can be corroded, maybe shorting out or unable to carry the behavior "current" for very long.

Using a concrete example, a universally stable motivation is to stay alive. We unconsciously tap into this when we swerve out of the way of another driver drifting into our lane. This light bulb is always fully wired and on. On the other end of the spectrum, a flickering light bulb of motivation may be our desire to declutter our desk—sometimes we do it, sometimes we don't—even if we always say we should. This wiring and light bulb may be more stable some days than others, depending on what other motivations are competing against it—outshining it.

Motivational wiring can carry the electricity, but it is not the electricity itself. Continuing the metaphor, if motivation is the wired light bulb, emotion is the electricity. Recall that we have identified emotion as the driver of decisions, the power behind action and the tipping point to behavior. It is the voltage that brings the motivation to light.

Just like electricity, emotion can happen with or without wiring. This means it can occur in free radical forms, like static shocks or lightning. These unwired surges of electrical power can ignite behavior change—but only if it is powerful, like lightning. We call these epiphanies, wake-up calls, and significant emotional events. This surge burns into our emotional memory an impression so impactful that we either stop a behavior (for example, getting sober after a tragic event like a car crash caused by a drunk driver) or actively seek out that behavior (for example, training even harder after winning a competition).

Emotional lightning bolts rarely change people for good, but it does happen. As physicians, we are often taught to scare people into epiphanies by saying things like, "Mr. Jones, if you don't stop doing X, you are going to die!" What is that except a surge of emotional energy to try to shock a patient into changing their behavior? And because it works infrequently, we do it often because we do not know what else to do since we really do not understand how motivation and emotion work.

When coupled with motivation, emotion is the current that brings the wiring to life and lights up the space. Without it, we can't make decisions and nothing holds our attention for very long. Therefore, emotion is the *more* we are speaking to when we say we need more motivation. When we say we need more motivation, we are really saying that we need to feel more, to pump up our emotions, in order to turn our light on and keep it on!

THE MOTIVATION-EMOTION 2×2

So how do we design using motivation and emotion? How do we stop using motivation in abstract terms?

How do we get emotions to work in our favor so that we start doing what we say we want to do? How do we build the circuit between motivation and emotions so our slow brain has a chance to beat our quick-triggered fast brain?

A popular tool in Silicon Valley, where I often teach and work, is the 2×2 table, which is a way of simplifying two things in relation to each other. So, I created a 2×2 table that would make it easy for you to think about emotion and motivation.

I hope by now I have at least partially convinced you that (a) emotion drives decisions, (b) people use the word *motivation* in ways that are vague and unhelpful when trying to change behavior, and (c) the neuroscience of both is super complex, therefore also unhelpful to a designer. My 2×2 table is a shortcut to designing for motivation and emotion. At the very least, I hope this matrix helps you go *aha* because you see motivation in a new light. But even more, I hope this becomes your new favorite tool when you think you have "to get more motivated."

The structure of this 2×2 is simple. Across the top, motivation is categorized into two types—stable or unstable. Down the left side, emotion is categorized into two types—strong or weak. This produces four quadrants, each with a unique combination: (1) stable motivation-strong emotion, (2) stable motivation-weak emotion, (3) unstable motivation-strong emotion, and (4) unstable motivation-weak emotion. (See figure 1.)

	STABLE MOTIVATION	**UNSTABLE MOTIVATION**
STRONG EMOTION	Stable motivation-Strong emotion 1	Unstable motivation-Strong emotion 3
WEAK EMOTION	2 Stable motivation-Weak emotion	4 Unstable motivation-Weak emotion

Figure 1. Motivation-Emotion 2x2 Table

Each of our life behaviors and experiences naturally falls into one of the quadrants. Take the stable motivation mentioned earlier of wanting to stay alive. That would also be a strong, lightning bolt-level emotion, so it would go under quadrant 1, behaviors and experiences that are characterized by stable motivations and strong emotions. The example of wanting to organize your desk is an unstable motivation most of the time and on the weak side emotionally speaking. It would go in quadrant 4. In fact, everything you do or want to motivate yourself to do fits into one of the four quadrants. I have grouped the types of themes and behavior patterns that correlate to each quadrant (figure 2), but I encourage you to do this for your own life behaviors—because only you know the truth about which of your motivations and emotions are strongest and weakest. There is a design exercise at the end of this chapter to do just that.

	STABLE MOTIVATION	UNSTABLE MOTIVATION
STRONG EMOTION	• Self-Image • Family/Social Connections • Survival • Safety/Self-Defense • Addictions • Purpose/Internal Rewards 1	3 • Inspirational • Awe • Wake-Up Calls • Vision Quest • Rehab/Recovery • External Rewards • Impulsivity/Life Drama
WEAK EMOTION	2 • Habit • Errands • Routines • Ruts/Norms • Biases	4 • To-Do Lists • New Year's Resolutions • Aspirations • Most Goal-Setting • Information/Education

Figure 2. Life's behaviors loaded into the Motivation-Emotion 2x2

This 2×2 table is a helpful design tool because it helps us figure out which behaviors will likely win out—either because they are stronger or more stable. For example, a fickle New Year's resolution in quadrant 4 is likely to get dominated by the strong emotions of life's drama, such as having a sick child, which would be a quadrant 3 category. You also may have a mind-blowing quadrant 3 experience, like hearing an inspirational speaker or going on a weekend spiritual retreat only to come back home and have all of your quadrant 2 daily habits slap you in the face and back into reality—forget quitting your job and starting your dream career, there are diapers to change! Finally, you may have a solid quadrant 2 habit of cleaning your house only to move in with a messy partner or roommate, and your quadrant 1 need for social connection gradually drags you into being more like them (or else it would drive you crazy).

You can now see that the quadrants follow a power hierarchy. They go in order of increasing levels of motivation-emotion and therefore the higher the motivation and emotion, the more those behaviors will win the battle of competing priorities. The strongest, most dominant behaviors live in quadrant 1, so quadrant 1 will almost always trump the others. The second most powerful is quadrant 2, then quadrant 3, and finally quadrant 4. (Notice how most of the new behaviors we want to start, like wanting to eat healthier, live in quadrant 4—just saying.)

So now let's talk about how to apply what we know from the 2×2 table using it as a design tool for our behavior change. Basically, you are going to do two things: (1) figure out which behaviors or habits are going to kick your new behavior's motivational ass because they are stronger emotionally or more stable motivationally, and (2) design a way to enhance your new behavior so it can compete against these stronger forces. Let's go through this quadrant-by-quadrant, so you can get to know each and learn how to use it as a designer.

QUADRANT 1
THE POWER GRID
(STABLE MOTIVATION WITH STRONG EMOTION)

Quadrant 1 certainly packs a punch, loaded with primal emotional and motivational life themes such as survival, connection to others, self-defense, and self-image. Every motivation light bulb in this category is either always on or easily flipped on as a fight or flight response. Emotions in this quadrant are high energy, reliable, and predictable—like a power grid—such as the love a healthy parent has for their children and their predictive self-sacrifice for them. This is the deep ocean of our values, our defense mechanisms, and our core temperament—people who know us well often find and push all these buttons. And while we might finesse the management of our actions and emotions as we mature, the initial triggers of our urges, cravings, and avoidances are with us for life (unless you meditate in a cave forever and become enlightened, of course). In this quadrant, we are pretty predictable. When the car in front of us brakes hard, we reflexively throw our arm out to protect the passenger. We return to our same addictions, whether media, food, or other pleasures. We actively promote and protect our personal self-image. If we can, we pick a safe neighborhood to raise our kids. Some things are essential—people always do the things in quadrant 1.

I like to say that this category of behavior is like solid ground. It is weight bearing. Therefore, whenever you design a new behavior, you want to try all that you can to ground that new behavior into the motivations and emotions of quadrant 1. If you can link your desired new behavior to themes of quadrant 1, it has a jump-start on survival and can ride the wave of forces that shape you as a person.

As I have said before, you are already designing your behavior and may not even know it. People intuitively tap into quadrant 1 themes all the time when they are trying to get themselves or others to adopt a new behavior. For example, many clinicians have figured out that patients do not want to take their medications—especially if it is for a painless condition like high cholesterol. So they invoke the power of quadrant 1 by asking the patient what they want to live for in the future. Then the patient might say, "well, I really want to be able to go to my daughter's wedding and be a grandparent someday." The clinician then leverages these quadrant 1 themes around survival and love for family and tells the patient that taking their medication will give them a better chance of living to experience those events. The patient, who previously had taken the cholesterol-lowering medication as maybe a to-do list item, which would be in quadrant 4, now has linked it to quadrant 1 and all its power. This is how you use the 2×2 table—by linking something hopeless like taking pills for which there is weak motivation to something more powerful like a daughter's wedding and grandbabies. What could be more powerful than grandbabies?! In this case, the concrete behavior design might be for the patient to place a picture of his daughter or other emotional reminder next to the medication.

What you are doing is taking a weaker emotion, like the *meh* of taking high-cholesterol medication, and piggybacking it on the solid, persistent emotions and motivations of quadrant 1. So, when you think *I just need to get more motivated*, the first thing you should do as a designer is see if you can dock it onto something in quadrant 1.

Recalling our previous example of aspirations to exercise more, when the people in my exercise survey said they didn't have time, we now know that it means that something in quadrant 1 was dominating the motivation-emotion of exercising behavior. Spending time with the kids, for example, was stronger emotionally and more stable motivationally than taking the time to exercise—and it sits 100 percent smack-dab in the middle of quadrant 1.

QUADRANT 2
SOLIDLY WIRED
(STABLE MOTIVATION WITH WEAK EMOTION)

Quadrant 2 is the second most powerful quadrant of behaviors. It holds all the autopilot behaviors of the fast brain as we discussed in chapter 3—our habits, routines, and shortcut biases. If you think about it, anything we do repeatedly and thoughtlessly must be driving off a stable motivation because the behavior is consistent, always on. We also don't power these behaviors with a lot of emotion—why waste energy on something as mundane as toothbrushing? These behaviors are so automated that all we need to spark the routine is the slightest feeling of tension or anxiety. For example, think of how you might use your smartphone. There is an underlying stable motivation to use your smartphone. The emotions that prompt you to use your smartphone are low-grade and have a weak current, but they are there. Wondering how your stock portfolio is doing? Check your stock app. Bored? Open a game app. Wondering what your friends are doing tonight? Open your Facebook app. Most of your smartphone use behaviors are quadrant 2 types.

So, if everything is on cruise control in quadrant 2, how do we use it to design a new behavior? This is where I really like Dr. Fogg's thinking. He is a big advocate of two methods that help link new behaviors to the power and consistency that lie in quadrant 2.

First, he suggests building a habit. He proposes to do this by sequencing the new behavior either before or right after an existing habit. As an example, if you brush your teeth every day twice a day, a new behavior may fit in right after that. Second, Dr. Fogg suggests taking baby steps to build a habit. This is smart because it matches the low emotional level needed to perform a repetitive routine. As a rule, the more ambitious the behavior, the more you would need the electricity of emotion to power it. That gets expensive for your brain, because we all know that burning high emotions all the time stresses us out and depletes our attention and decision capacity. It's exhausting! Therefore, when designing you can leverage quadrant 2 by creating small habits and piggybacking them on existing habits, as Dr. Fogg has discovered.

Another helpful tip for quadrant 2 behaviors comes from my favorite naturalist mentor, Jon Young. Jon is big on his students establishing awareness routines, especially morning routines. He advocates for an ancient indigenous practice of morning meditation in nature that includes feeling gratitude and observing the behavior patterns of birds and animals. This practice helps his students develop a 360-degree awareness of their immediate environment, as well as an awareness of the interplay of cause and effect relationships within the ecosystem, which helps them build pattern awareness.

I followed his method for two years, getting up at dawn to sit out in front of my suburban house and record in my journal all the bird and animal behavior I saw. Rain or shine, I was outside at 6:00 a.m. on my front lawn sitting on the ground, listening and recording in my journal what I experienced. By thinking of this bird study as my morning routine, I was able to put it on cruise control, even though it was initially a strange, new behavior. Because I had designed the new behavior as a quadrant 2 daily activity, a morning routine, it lasted under that protection and stability for years, until we moved out of that house.

QUADRANT 3
LIGHTNING BOLTS
(UNSTABLE MOTIVATION WITH STRONG EMOTION)

Have you ever gone to an event, like to hear a motivational speaker or to participate in a workshop, that excited and inspired you so much that you just *knew* you would go back home and immediately change your whole life forever? Upon re-entry through your front door, however, did you have to instead immediately clean up dog poo or handle a screaming child or grumpy spouse? Did you have a big stack of bills or e-mails that yanked you right back down to earth? Were you back to your old self within a week? For most people, this describes the power and fall from a quadrant 3 experience: lightning-like emotion mixed with flickering and unstable motivation afterward. What happened?

Quadrants 1 and 2 happened. You see, building a new behavior on an unstable motivation is like building your house on shifting ground. The unstable motivation of quadrant 3 (and quadrant 4, for that matter) are as ephemeral as the surface waves on the ocean—sometimes they are there, sometimes they are not. The quadrant 3 motivations are smaller unstable waves compared to the powerful stable motivations of quadrants 1 and 2. And smaller waves get consumed by larger ones. This is the nature of unstable motivation—it is dynamic, impermanent, and very unreliable. Like the faulty wiring and light bulb metaphor we covered earlier, an unstable motivation flickers on and off.

Don't get me wrong, quadrant 3 can sometimes change your life. Sometimes you *do* come home from the inspirational speaker and leave your dysfunctional relationship, quit your job, or start that company you always wanted (I have done all three). I am a huge fan of passion-based decisions, so quadrant 3 is a comfy home base for me. However, the issue with relying on quadrant 3 to change behavior is that you never know what is going to happen—or how long the strong emotion will last. When people have a heart attack, they often call it their wake-up call. But if you look at their behavior after they survive, less than half of them change one healthy thing permanently and 25 percent do not try to change at all.[30] And that's a life-threatening heart attack! Therefore, it is not a given that a quadrant 3 lightning bolt of emotion, realization, or wake-up call will change your behavior. As a designer, you have to experiment with when, how, and how much to use it—remember that you are playing with lightning.

So, here is how I think of it. Quadrant 3 should be your go-to design quadrant whenever you are *meh* about making a change. If you feel ambivalent, stuck, apathetic, uninspired, or defeated, look to quadrant 3 for ideas of how to amp up your emotions. The movie "*Yes*

Man" with Jim Carrey is a perfect example of how one man uses quadrant 3 experiences to change his behavior and life (notice he also uses a quadrant 2 routine/algorithm of saying yes to everything). It is like a perk-me-up cup of coffee when you are dragging. If you hear yourself saying "I just need to get more motivated" and you can't quite dock your new behavior into quadrant 1 and you know you do not yet care enough to bother with designing a routine to tap into the power of quadrant 2, then design for quadrant 3. Look for sources of inspiration and awe, and wake-up calls. Seek out exhilaration, risk, novelty, meaning, and passion. Awaken your creativity through dance classes or pottery classes. Sign up for a Tough Mudder. Go on a silent spiritual retreat. Go travel. Whatever it is that will wake you out of your sleepy, anhedonic, paralyzed state. Quest!

I make it my practice to do an annual solo quest. This usually entails going out into remote wilderness completely away from people—in fact, I avoid them entirely—for five to six days. I do not bring food, only iodine tablets to purify my water and a granola bar to eat, for energy when I am heading back. This is my quadrant 3. By intentionally designing an annual dose of *aha* into my life, I find that I never lack strong emotion or suffer flickering motivation to implement what I learn on my quest.

This may be too extreme for most people, but it also can be done in miniature. New research by Dr. Dacher Keltner of the UC Berkeley Greater Good Science Center shows that just having people stare at a grove of tall trees for five minutes causes them to feel a sense of awe, more inspired, more collaborative, and more generous than a control group who stared at a tall building for five minutes.[31] This means that you can stimulate what you need in quadrant 3 in just a few minutes—and possibly use the power of that emotion to nudge your little motivation ball over the edge to accelerate down the ramp.

QUADRANT 4
STATIC SHOCKS & SPARKS
(UNSTABLE MOTIVATION WITH WEAK EMOTION)

Quadrant 4 contains all the little things that we say we'd like to do, almost in an offhand or even wishful way. "I want to lose 10 pounds." "I hope to go to Fiji someday." "I want to try skydiving." They are fleeting ideas that come and go and get easily dominated and lost in the deep ocean waves of stronger emotions and super-stable motivations. Or they are things we do for a little while but die out easily—once again, like New Year's resolutions.

For a new behavior that has unstable, flickering motivation and passing emotions, the best design boost is to anchor it to one of the stronger quadrants to power behavior change. You can dial up the emotion by incorporating a quadrant 3 experience and see if it catches fire from there. You also can try to routinize it like a quadrant 2 behavior and see if it will "graft" onto one of the other habits and routines in your life. You can also add temporary stability by giving it a time limit as a quadrant routine even though you know it will not last. An example would be giving up something for Lent (only 40 days) or intensely studying for the week before a final exam. Finally, you can see if it will dock into any of your quadrant 1 behaviors or themes; simply list out your quadrant 1 themes and see if any of them can be linked to your quadrant 4 aspirational behavior.

Remember, this is an iterative process, like how I find the right blue piece in the ocean section within a large jigsaw puzzle—by trying all four edges of one blue piece, then trying another one and so forth. Keep in mind that your schedule is packed with things that are strongly emotional or motivationally stable. The only way an unstable motivation, as in quadrant 4, is going to survive is to reinforce it with the power of the other quadrants.

HOW THIS RELATES TO OTHER MODELS

There are many motivational models and theories and discoveries. The 2×2 table we just learned about is a design tool, rather than a motivation theory, that cuts to the chase. At the same time, it is consistent with everything I have studied. Specifically, I think it adds dimension to two of the more popular models of behavior change: the social determinants of health and Maslow's hierarchy of needs.

In the social determinants of health model, a person's health and health choices are shaped by the backdrop of their life.[32] In other words, social, environmental, and economic factors influence how healthy a person is. According to public health and health economics, it explains why some people are healthier than other people: competing motivations! This supports the 2×2 table we just learned about; competing motivations is another way of describing how more stable motivations will beat out those less stable to express behaviors. Now, translating this to add the emotional dimension, some people have both a ton of competing motivations and strong negative emotions. Their life drama and stress ultimately dominates their attention and represses their healthy motivations.

For example, I once toured a highly successful Medicaid program center for seniors in Philadelphia. Their executive director shared with me real stories of what they face when caring for their community's most vulnerable elderly. He described one elderly woman who had her door stolen right off the hinges! That was the day that she missed her doctor appointment. Of course, she had a quadrant 1 problem. Her strongest emotion and most stable motivation at that moment was safety, which meant that getting a new door dominated the motivation for taking care of her health that day. The center staff was smart—and so was their funding agency. They used a portion of the money they received for her care to buy and install a new front door.

Another popular model, the classic story of psychology's view on motivation, begins with Maslow's hierarchy of needs. In the early 1940s, psychologist Abraham Maslow proposed how motivation works in a hierarchical fashion. He posited that there are simple and more complex motivations, and that a person has to satisfy their lower, more base-level needs first. Basic survival-oriented physiological needs form the base of the motivational pyramid; without food and water, we die—there is no negotiating around that! Then the hierarchy of needs progresses up through safety needs (including physical and financial security), love and belongingness needs (including family and intimacy), and esteem needs (including respect and recognition). Finally, and some psychologists argue that very few people resolve the final need, we have self-actualization needs. This is the achievement of one's own personal best, or, as Maslow put it, "what people can be, they must be."[33]

Aligned with Maslow, our 2×2 table design tool is a more dynamic system, describing the on/off flow of emotional "electricity" and the flickering and variable brightness of some motivation wires or bulbs over others. The 2×2 table gives a more predictive picture of which behaviors will dominate, given what quadrant they are in. But unlike Maslow's hierarchy and more like the competing priorities of social determinants of health, the 2×2 table embraces the rising and falling of individual waves of emotion and motivation that may temporarily cause a quadrant 4 behavior to beat a quadrant 1 behavior. This takes a lot of the self-flogging out of the need to get more motivated because now we understand the definition of motivation as a moving, shifting system of competing emotions and motivations. There are no absolutes, just context and dynamics. And that's why it is important—because if we are beating ourselves up over our "lack of motivation," then we have even less motivation. My hope is that the 2×2 table frees you from any harmful ways you may have been using motivation—and empowers you to just design for increasing motivation—according to how it exists in nature!

I am so cheering you on.

My 2×2 Table

Here are a few exercises to work on with your own motivation-emotion 2×2 table.

1. Take your personal 2×2 inventory. To really get at how motivation and emotion are operating on a personal level, I find it helpful to ask the kinds of questions organized by quadrant below. Remember that this is all about you and your behaviors and experiences, so answer as few or many questions as you would like.

	STABLE MOTIVATION	UNSTABLE MOTIVATION
STRONG EMOTION	• What are your core self-images? • How do family and social connections influence your behavior the most? • What makes you go into survival mode? When that happens, what do you do? • What makes you feel unsafe and defensive? What do you do most often? • What are your addictions? • What gives you a sense of purpose? • What do you find internally rewarding?	• When have you been really, really inspired? • What behaviors did you change or try to change when that happened? • Where do you find a sense of awe? How does that shift your behavior? • What wake-up calls have you had? • What vision quests or seeking have you done? • When have you gone into rehabilitation or recovery? What was it like? • In what ways are you pursuing external rewards? • When do you participate in impulsivity? Life drama?
	1	3
	2	4
WEAK EMOTION	• What are your primary habits? • What errands are typical for you? • What morning, evening, and weekend routines do you have? • What rituals do you follow? • What are your ruts, where you feel stuck doing the same thing? • What is "normal" for you? • What biases do you see in yourself? • What assumptions and judgments do you typically make?	• What is your motivational relationship with to-do lists? What emotions do they bring up? • What New Year's resolutions have you made in the past? • What are your aspirations, even those you do not share openly? • What kind of goal-setting doesn't work for you? What does work? How long does it tend to work? • When does learning new information or acquiring education help you? When does it fail to help you?

2. Fill in the following sentences to learn how to strengthen the motivation and emotion of a new behavior design.

I feel motivated to design a new behavior for

_____

(name your behavior change), which I think

fits into my quadrant _____

(1, 2, 3, or 4) because it has _____

(stable/unstable) motivation and _____
(strong/weak) emotion. One way I can
strengthen my design using the 2×2 table

would be to draw from quadrant _____
(1, 2, 3, or 4) because I could use the

emotion of _____
(name a stronger emotion from that quadrant)

and the motivation of _____

(name a more stable motivation from that quadrant) to help make my behavior more likely to succeed. I can leverage the energy of

quadrant _____ (fill in the

stronger quadrant) by _____ (reminding myself of the theme/setting up a routine/increasing my emotion) with

_____

(how you will do this).

Notes

⑥

design for lasting change

Never give up.
No matter what!

—David Lewis

Delivering wisdom through stories has been practiced by native people since time immemorial. A Native American elder told this story of two wolves to his young grandson:

> "A great battle rages inside of me every day, Grandson."
>
> "What do you mean, Grandfather?"
>
> The grandfather responded, "There are two wolves that fight ferociously for power.

One is a mean wolf. He knows anger, greed, gossip, jealousy, and revenge. He is proud and untrustworthy.

"The other is a wolf of lightness. He lives in joy, peace, generosity, love, and laughter, and he brings out these gentle qualities in others. Every day, these wolves fight with each other. Everyone has these two wolves living inside of them."

The young boy remained thoughtfully silent for a while. Then he questioned, "Tell me, Grandfather, which wolf will win?"

"Grandson, the wolf you feed."

More than just a fable, this ancient story describes what happens in our brain when we change our behavior. It offers us a helpful mental model for how we can sustain new behaviors—by recognizing that there is a fierce competition between the new and old inside of us. The story of the battling wolves reflects how our brain is wired and, more importantly, the role we must play to rewire it and maintain the behaviors we desire.

One of my pet peeves has been the spreading of the urban myth that it takes three weeks to establish a new habit. It has become a commonly held belief, but it is not true. Few people know that this myth came from a guess made by a plastic surgeon, Dr. Maxwell Maltz, in 1960, and was based on how long he thought it took his patients to adjust to their new nose job.[34] He guessed! And as a result, decades of well-meaning people have used it as a rule of thumb (yep, a heuristic) to their detriment. Trusting this adage from Maltz, good people work their butts off for the 21 days they think is required, and then they think it's a done deal only to relapse to the old behavior soon afterwards. What's worse is that they blame themselves because they think they did something wrong or they were too weak to keep up the new habit. Their habenula counts one against them, and they stop trying. But they were operating from Maltz's pseudoscientific guess. It breaks my heart.

So, let's set the record straight about how long it takes to build a new habit and how to really keep it going!

NEUROPLASTICITY

Neuroscientists used to believe that the adult brain was an unchanging landscape. It was thought that tremendous growth and change happened only during childhood—with prolific connections forming between neurons that became pruned with bonsai-like precision—but that these processes leveled off and stopped by adolescence. And then, well, you were left with what you had. It's as good as it gets and there's nowhere to go from there but downhill. You can't teach an old dog new tricks!

One of the neuroscientists that changed this view was Donald Hebb.[35] His theory of Hebbian learning describes how neurons in the brain form neural networks through repeated actions, like when you memorize lyrics to a song through listening to it over and over. When a thought or behavior is repeated, it gets reinforced in the anatomy and chemistry of the brain, giving it more potential to occur again in the future. Later on, newer technologies like the functional MRI that can view brain activity via blood flow helped validate Hebb's theory. This concept is now famous to millions and has lent itself to this catch phrase: Neurons that fire together wire together.

In other words, the wolf that gets fed the most, wins.

Furthermore, the process of neurons wiring together from repeated use and learning, called neuroplasticity, has been found to happen not just in childhood but at any and every age! What is now understood about the brain is that it is an ever-changing, dynamic system. It is constantly rewiring itself. Old, unused "wires" (neural circuits) are clipped or fall into disrepair. For example, you might meet someone and think, *Oh, oh. I know her face, but I can't remember her name*, which means that that neural network might be a little rusty. In contrast, freshly used wires constantly are reinforced and strengthened. For example, your address is always easily accessible because you use it to pay bills, direct visitors, and verify purchases.

BACK TO THE WOLVES

In wolf packs, there is always an alpha wolf, the leader of the pack. They are the strongest, most dominant single wolf, and the rest of the wolves defer to them. Sometimes a young wolf gets the notion that he or she wants to lead the pack. They challenge the alpha. Fighting ensues, and the winner gets to lead. Let's use what we know about alpha wolves as a metaphor for neuroplasticity and go through the steps of behavior change in the brain.

Using the wolves metaphor, we will cover the four phases of neuroplasticity, all of which last a predictable amount of time.

PHASE 1
THE FIRST WEEK[36]

Your old behavior is the alpha of your pack, your default behavior because it is so strong and established. Let's say your alpha wolf old behavior is that you eat a bagel with cream cheese for breakfast pretty much every day. When you design a new behavior—in this case maybe you want to switch to a healthy breakfast of Greek yogurt with unsweetened granola—it is like adding a newborn baby wolf to the pack. During its youth, the baby wolf is protected from the alpha and fed by his mother—this protection and feeding is done in the brain by your attention span. As long as its mother continues to feed and protect the baby wolf (i.e., your attention span continues to focus on doing the new behavior—eating Greek yogurt), he or she will grow and get stronger.

The baby wolf can be likened to a newly formed, loosely wired neural network in your brain. This new neural network builds strength through repetition—the repetition that is afforded by sustained attention. And just as the baby wolf would die without the continual nurturing from its mother, your newly formed neural network easily shrivels if your attention lapses. This first phase of building a new neural network in the brain takes only one week, but these new neural connections quickly die if they are not fed.

PHASE 2
UP TO THREE MONTHS[37]

Our baby wolf (behavior) grows into an adolescent, which means that it reaches maximum height but not weight. In neuroplasticity terms, the new behavior's neural network is fully connected but is still what is called gray matter (which in the brain is the color of new growth and networking). You have eaten a lot of Greek yogurt to get to this point, and you are pretty consistent. The adolescent wolf is strong enough to start fending for itself, yet not strong enough to lead the pack. This means that the behavior we started has some strength but is not fully matured to the level of our old alpha behavior. The protection and food starts to shift from the mother to the adolescent wolf, but the young wolf still needs to gain strength.

Note that it can take up to three months to establish an adolescent wolf, or full-sized neural network. Three months—not three weeks—and even then, we are not done.

PHASE 3
UP TO ONE YEAR[38, 39]

If our wolf (behavior), through repeatedly being fed and protected by our attention span, lives to be a full-height adolescent, then it is time for it to add girth and weight. In the brain, the equivalent to our adolescent wolf packing on weight is myelination. Neural networks that are repeated enough for long enough get myelinated. Myelin is a substance that the brain adds to coat the neural networks that are used most often. It insulates the electric signal carried by these networks so they can move much faster (exactly, they join the fast brain!). There is a range for when this phase is done,[40] but it can take up to one year, just as an adolescent wolf growing into full adult girth takes at least a full year. Your brain is basically acknowledging that the Greek yogurt thing is here to stay.

Once the adolescent wolf has become a full-fledged adult member of the pack, things get interesting. First of all, our newly adult wolf challenges the old alpha wolf to lead—to dominate our expressed behavior. In breakfast terms, this means that you aim to fully replace bagels with Greek yogurt and never look back—Greek yogurt would become alpha. But for the young wolf to be strong enough to do this, it has to keep up the food intake—from our attention. Is it still the upstart wolf we feed or do we feed the old default alpha wolf? Our newly adult wolf is not a cute little baby wolf anymore, so our attention span may turn to feed new projects (such as getting ourselves to eat a healthy lunch) or may even get distracted or stressed and forget to feed the newly adult wolf. This adult wolf, aka healthy breakfast, goes through feast or famine corresponding with the stability of our attention. Some days our new adult wolf is winning the battle, and other days the old alpha gets fed and wins the battle.

Hypocrisy ensues. Maybe one day you are eating Greek yogurt, then on another day you grab a bagel because bagels were served at the morning work meeting. Hypocrisy, or pledging to do A but then actually doing B, is the ultimate expression of the battle between two wolves. It is actually a sign of the two wolves fighting over food: the attention span. Many people hate seeing hypocrisy in their behavior. But it can be a sign of progress—you grew a wolf big enough to challenge the alpha! Yay, you! Instead of giving up, it is a sign to double down on feeding the new challenger wolf and weakening the old reigning alpha.

This is where design helps. We can design to give advantages to the newly adult wolf. We can use design to make it easier to feed the new alpha wolf and make it harder to feed the old alpha wolf. For example, we could buy Greek yogurt in bulk and buy a bunch of favorite toppings so it is all we have around the house in the morning. Therefore, if we have supports in place— friends, environments, designs—the new alpha wolf continues to be fed and triumphs over the old alpha wolf. Our new behavior wins over the old bad habit.

PHASE 4
THE REST OF OUR LIFE[41, 42]

Here is how the two wolves story plays out over the long term. Recall from chapter 1 that every design has an expiration date? This means that our newly adult wolf, challenger to the alpha, must receive redesigns (iterations) from time to time to refresh the attention it gets and must continue to be fed the most. In our wolf metaphor, this also means that the battle between the wolves never ends—and this is where using neuroplasticity to understand behavior change helps us.

In our brain, the old alpha, the myelinated neural network that supported our old behavior, never dies.

True, it may get weakened or dominated, even semiretired. But where I see most behavior change methods fail people, is when they think, *ding-dong, the old alpha wolf is dead* and the newly adult wolf is the permanent winner. Wrong—the alpha wolf can always come back—and he does! The old alpha wolf is called a relapse.

Relapse is a loaded term. For most people, especially those in the addiction community, it holds a daunting meaning. Certainly, in cases like heroin addiction where a relapse could mean life or death, it should be respected for the seriousness it warrants. However, I want to diminish the gravity of relapse for the vast majority of behaviors that are not life threatening.

Many people suffer needlessly when they change their behavior, feed and raise their new wolf to take over, only to see the old alpha wolf make a comeback. They say to themselves, *what's the point? I failed.* Instead, I want them to think, *OK, so I relapsed. What is this teaching me and how can I feed the new wolf more?* I want relapse to be a symptom that simply reminds people to nonjudgmentally self-diagnose and reignite their efforts. Let's make relapse be a helpful feedback loop for ourselves as designers. Relapse is not bad, it is just an alarm that points to where your design has leaks or maybe has started to expire and crumble.

LONG-TERM CHANGE

So what does it take to change behavior and make it stick long term? Many experts have taken a crack at this question by creating numerous theories, models, books, and courses. For some of the people some of the time, these strategies do work, so it is good to have such choices available. But I have found that the only thing that changes behavior in the long term is engagement, which is built from sustained attention and a supportive environment. Thinking about the phases of neuroplasticity we just covered, this makes sense—sustained attention always feeds the good wolf, and the supportive environment keeps the old bad wolf from coming back.

I have observed that people naturally tend to go through a cycle with their attention. First, they discover something really cool and they rave about it. They do that cool thing for period of time, then get bored or tired with it. They may even age out of it, like in a sport such as gymnastics. Then they move on to something else. Most of the time, they are not being flaky (although that can be the case for some) because some people's attention span could be decades long. Instead, people are simply expressing the story of the two wolves—the dynamic need for contrast, the reality that life is changing, or maybe the body is aging. Whatever the reason, we know that our designs will expire. And what is it exactly that expires? Our attention!

DESIGNING FOR ATTENTION

OK, so by now we know that there is a competition in the brain between our old (undesirable) behavior and the new behavior we built through repetition and neuroplasticity. In our story of neuroplasticity, we know that raising a new wolf means that the wolf lives and dies by how much we repeat and sustain our attention—this is how we feed it. We also know that if our attention lapses over time and we stop feeding it, our new wolf will lose.

Therefore, in basic brain terms, long-term behavior change is just a by-product of long-term repeat attention. But how do we keep our own attention? We design for it, of course!

In designing to get and hold our attention, let's start with the conscious, slow-brain attention, or the "I know that I know" feeling. In conscious attention, we can intentionally direct what we pay attention to—for example, carefully counting calories. However, this form of attention, because it burns precious slow-brain resources, gets bored very easily—especially with repetition. This is called desensitization. We ignore redundant things and move them to our unconscious when there is no contrast. This helps us save energy for novel things like sudden threats or new opportunities.

And therein lies the rub! We need the repetition of our slow-brain attention to feed and grow the new wolf, and yet our attention wanes the more we repeat the same behavior. We are no different from a child who begs their parents for a puppy and once they get one loses interest so the puppy becomes the parents' responsibility. Trying to grab and keep the conscious attention engaged is similar to getting a baby to smile for a picture—we end up jumping up and down like a clown, trying a million different squeak toys to get them to look at us, and even that may last only a second. What to do?

Designing a way to grab our slow-brain attention usually falls into one of two strategies: setting up external triggers or using mental algorithms. My mentor, naturalist Jon Young, builds external triggers into all of his awareness-training programs. In his beginner course, Kamana, he suggests that students train their awareness by noticing trees as a trigger to remember to be aware in the moment. Other courses I know of use the breath as a trigger to relax, a rubber band snap on the wrist to bring awareness, or even a sensation like hunger as a trigger to pay attention to what one eats. The external trigger can be an object, an event, a person, or a sensation, as long as it effectively draws the attention.

You can also imagine that the frequency of the trigger has to be just right. If it comes too often, your brain will desensitize; too seldom and you might end up thinking *oh yeah, that's that thing that was supposed to remind me to do* X. Just like all designs, a trigger expires and needs to be refreshed. In fact, I find that a lot of relapse happens as my old trigger is no longer getting my attention and I haven't yet designed a new one. I once heard author and blogger Nir Eyal say that the best triggers come from our social networks because they offer a constant stream of fresh external triggers that grab our attention. This is why online communities full of eye candy like Instagram or Pinterest are so addictive that we struggle to pull away.

Another way to grab the attention of our conscious mind is through using mental algorithms. An algorithm is a set of rules for solving a problem. A common way to express this is by using the format "if this then that," meaning that if X happens then do Y. People who are effective at designing their behaviors use mental algorithms that are simple and portable. For example, one of my company's founding designers, Andrew, made an astute observation during one of his design projects where he was helping people with diabetes shop for food. He notes that those who were good at controlling their blood sugar used highly specific shopping algorithms, such as not buying any food that had over a certain number of grams of sugar.

Why do these algorithms work? They help our slow brain mimic our fast brain. They grab our attention under certain conditions, act fast, and then go away—leaving our slow brain intact. Eventually, if used enough, these algorithms that are initially designed by the slow brain become fast-brain myelinated superhighways.

DESIGNING FOR OUR ENVIRONMENT

Now, let's figure out how to manage the unconscious attention of our fast brain, what we could call the notion of not knowing that we know. I say manage because, by definition, we do not control it willfully. But we still can—and absolutely must—design for it. Recall that our fast brain implicit memory tracks nearly everything that happens to and around us. It detects patterns before we know there are any and shapes our behaviors long before our conscious mind figures it out. Like a sponge, our implicit memory is constantly absorbing everything our eyes, ears, and other senses take in. It pays attention, even when we consciously don't.

Our environment grabs the attention of our fast brain. Our house, our community, our technology devices, our friends—they all trigger our unconscious mind constantly. If we ignore this fact, pretty soon our old alpha wolf of bad habits will be leading the pack again! In my own research of health habits of families, I have witnessed over and over again how spouses influence each other and how parents influence their kids. A person with food addictions can drag her spouse down into that world too. On the flip side, a person who is very healthy can pull their spouse up into a healthier way of living. Some people even start to design their partner's behavior, especially when there is a medical issue like diabetes.

For instance, one man I met shared his struggle with diabetes and how his doctor urged him to stop eating cookies. He told me the only reason he stopped was because his wife stepped in and took control of all the grocery shopping and didn't buy cookies anymore. He had cut back to eating only the cookies his adult daughter brought when she visited.

What was more interesting was my conversation with his wife. You see, she knew her husband had zero control if there were cookies around and she loved him so much she didn't want to lose him to an early death. So she secretly bought a box of mini-cookies and stored a small handful of them in sandwich Ziploc bags way in the back of her closet. Then when her daughter would come to visit, she would slip her daughter one of the baggies of cookies. The daughter then walked in, "Hey, Dad! I brought you some cookies." Meanwhile, the cookies were in the house the whole time, hidden from him all along. The beloved husband felt good because he was getting a treat. He felt supported that his wife, for his health, had banned cookies in the house. And the clever wife designed a way to make him happy and connect him with his daughter in a fun way. This is a perfect example of how important it is to design our environment—to manage the attention our fast brain pays to the everyday triggers, like the presence or absence of cookies.

We humans have always been social animals. In this story and many stories like it the pattern is clear: long-term sustained change requires a design of the environment, whether people, places, or things. In almost no instance in my research was a lone person able to change

their behavior *and sustain it* if their environment or
family did not in some way change with them. This also
illustrates why special behaviors, like meal plans or one
person eating differently than the rest of the group, is not
sustainable.

This pattern of how our personal relationships
unconsciously shape our attention has been validated
by many research studies. The Framingham Heart
Study is an ongoing study that started in Framingham,
Massachusetts in 1948 and has since tracked the health
of three generations—thousands of participants. Because
of such a big sample size, these results have been instrumental in establishing connections among cardiovascular disease, weight gain, and dietary and other social/
environmental variables through the years. Over 2,600
studies have been published based on this data set as of
the printing of this book. Many studies have focused on
predicting who will develop cardiovascular disease and,
of course, how both environment and genetics play an
important role.[43]

Framingham and other long-term health-tracking
studies offer proof of how our environment serves as a
giant field of triggers for our unconscious attention. For
example, the Framingham data have shown that there

is a sort of network effect in obesity.[44] An individual's chance of being obese is elevated by 57 percent if they have a close friend who is also obese—even if they had moved away years before! This effect is even stronger than it is with siblings, an observation that shows that environmental influences, such as peer relationships, can trump genes.

If one person in a family is obese, there is a 40 percent increase in the probability of their siblings becoming obese. Similarly, spousal rates of obesity were correlated at 37 percent. All of this can be explained by how our environment, including our closest relation-ships, grabs the attention of our unconscious mind—our old alpha wolf is fed by our environment and everyone in it.

Given these compelling patterns, it is of utmost importance that we design our environment if we are to sustain our behavior change in the long term. Think of your environment as a trigger field—everything you see, touch, feel, smell, and hear triggers you one way or another. Everything feeds one wolf or the other. If you think of it this way, you see the importance of using design to lower and remove the bad triggers, like the wife who removed cookies for her husband, and increase the good triggers, like the same wife buying all healthy groceries.

There are two classic models for this: cold turkey and harm reduction. Alcoholics Anonymous teaches people to design using the cold turkey model by removing every single trigger that is alcohol-related, such as hanging out with drinking buddies, taking even one sip, and even walking by bars.

Going cold turkey gets trickier, however, if your addiction is food because you have to eat. In this case, the harm reduction route may help. Harm reduction helps people replace old addictive triggers gradually. It involves the tapering off of something, like drinking smaller cans of soda, as well as switching to better alternatives, like substituting fruit-infused soda water for soda.

BEATING THE BIG BAD WOLF

With any new behavior expect to get distracted by old patterns and relapse. This is so normal; it's inevitable, really. Don't fret! We will cover how to bounce back from relapse in chapter 9. Steady progress toward sustained behavior change has nothing to do with the old behavior rearing its ugly head from time to time. It means that you keep your attention on the new desired behavior and work toward increasing the time between relapsing into the undesired behavior.

I did this with fast food. I grew up in Oklahoma, where there were tons of fast-food places. My family would go to McDonald's after church on Sundays. Years later, when I was a teenager with a car and spending cash from my job at the local mall, I suddenly had power and freedom! My reward to myself when I was done with work was to hit the drive-through and buy whatever I wanted. Fast forward to the college years, I kept eating fast food. And this continued into my 20s. Only when I tried to stop eating fast food did I realize how much of a problem I had because I couldn't stop.

I realized that for me, fast food was wired to all kinds of things. It was fully baked into my attention span because I thought about it often and looked forward to when I could have it again. It was a reward. It was down-home. It was the old alpha wolf. And it was all over my environment. Yikes! That's potent stuff to unwire. And it has taken me more than 20 years to starve that wolf.

Here's what I have noticed about the pattern of my long-term behavior change from eating fast food. After more than 20-plus years of removing fast food from my life, I would still relapse when I was stressed, rushed, tired, or when it was late at night and better restaurants or grocery stores were closed. I would also relapse when I didn't have a dinner plan for my kids or our errand running took us past their mealtime, and a nearby fast-food place offered a quick fix.

But the most interesting thing was that each year that went by, I found myself going for longer and longer intervals before I would relapse. At first I couldn't make it a week without fast food, then I stretched it to a month in between relapses, then eventually six months. As of today, the last time I had fast food was two years ago. It was a by-product of continuing to refocus my attention and shift my environment. If I noticed my attention fixating on the fast food, I would go to a healthier restaurant instead. Over time, I trained my brain not to "see" fast-food restaurants.

From this decades-long behavior design experiment on myself, I can tell you that the two wolves are real. Relapse is real. Taking longer than three weeks to change behavior is real. But so is designing and redesigning and never, ever giving up.

To sum it all up, here is some practical, pithy advice for putting the concepts from this chapter into action:

- Expect to endure competition from the old default behavior. The wolves are battling. Your job is to feed the right one.

- Manage your attention by designing and redesigning (iterating) to keep yourself engaged in change. This includes only changing behaviors that you can continue to pay attention to—too many changes will fracture your attention. For example, if you were remodeling your home on a budget, you wouldn't rip up the entire house and get started on everything simultaneously. You can only design as much as you have in your slow brain's attention budget. Manage your attention as carefully as you would manage a budget. Just like the wolf story, the behavior you see is merely a function of the attention you feed it.

- Remember to design your environment to feed the wolf you want. This means removing or reducing unconscious triggers for the old alpha wolf and replacing them with new triggers, people, places, or things that feed the new wolf.

Over decades of changing behavior, others and my own, I have obsessed over why we do what we do, and, more interestingly, why we don't do what we know we should do. This search has led me to the brain and how it responds to efforts to change it. Now *you* know what the brain really does over time. Now *you* know what to do and how long it takes to change. You also know how to make it last and how to keep feeding it. Most importantly, you know that it's normal for the old alpha wolf to rear his head—and no big deal. You know what that means now. You are not confused anymore. You know that you can remain calm and just start feeding the new wolf again.

Design Your Attention

Here are some guiding exercises that I have found helpful in designing an environment to be supportive of new behaviors:

> Name three things in your environment that you think need to be redesigned to support the change you want in your life. These may be specific locations, negative triggers, certain types of people, or other factors.

> 1. _____

> 2. _____

> 3. _____

> What would you change about each of them in order to support your new behavior design?

> 1. _____

> 2. _____

3. _____

How could you make those changes?

_____

_____

_____

_____

_____

_____

_____

_____

_____

If you feel like it is the right time, pick something (small and easy) from your list and design it for change—either with an environmental trigger or an internal algorithm.

Notes

⑦

track your damn self

Until you make the unconscious conscious, it will direct your life and you will call it fate.

—C. G. Jung

B ritt Johnson is saving every one of her prescription pain medicine bottles for what she imagines one day will be an art installation. This is just one reflection of her courageous approach to her disease—severe, debilitating chronic pain from multiple forms of auto-immune arthritis and migraines, first onset at age seven. Britt is the consummate behavior designer, approaching her condition with the mindset of iterative design. She says: "Figuring out how to manage my disease is always a work in progress. I tinker on myself like an old man tinkers on his beloved classic car. Lovingly finding ways to care for it, finding just the right parts to keep it functional, and taking it out for a spin in the Sunday sunshine." (Britt, from her blog, www.thehurtblogger.com)

Britt poetically shares such deep insights into her behavior and experiences through her blog. This is where she chronicles her ongoing struggles with pain, medications, insurance coverage, and life in general to the benefit of fellow pain patients, physicians, and other followers. An e-patient advocate, she works as a medical consultant to promote patient-centered care and design in healthcare systems and technology. I first met her through Dr. Larry Chu, with whom I teach health engagement and design courses at Stanford. She is a brilliant woman, who is using design to improve health and healthcare for herself and others.

Britt writes openly on her site about periodic flare-ups and migraines of such severity that they sometimes land her in the emergency room. On a daily basis, she deals with levels of pain that most of us cannot even fathom, but sometimes even she has to seek help. She may be the first to fault herself for dealing with the pain "too well." Or at least she found out that she was underestimating the pain level that she was communicating to emergency room physicians. When asked the traditional assessment question of how she would rate her pain on a scale of 1 to 10, Britt would answer 6, causing the physicians not to take her seriously. But a 6 for Britt is more like a 9 for a normal person because her chronic suffering had built up stoicism in her from a young age. But this stoicism backfired when she really needed to get help because to an ER doc a 6 score puts Britt in the low urgency, back burner category. She needed a better way to communicate her experience.

After several flare-ups and ER visits, Britt was asked by her physicians to self-track her pain with a pain scale at home. Self-tracking is a process of collecting data on one's health and behaviors to gain insights into cause and effect patterns that can hopefully inform a better approach. It is a foundational practice for designing behaviors. Britt knows it quite well, having been confronted with pain scales in doctors' offices since she was a young girl. These pain scales typically show a 1–10 scale of progressively happy to miserable facial expressions with descriptive words for each level, like Worst Pain Possible for the 10. But for Britt, and many chronic pain patients, this type of scale misses the mark. Such chronic pain patients probably are prone to giving a lower rating to their daily pain than someone who is experiencing an acute new pain and doesn't have all the years of adapting, accepting, and adjusting. In other words, for those with chronic pain, their sense of *Me* includes being in constant pain, whereas another person would reject the pain as *Not Me*—thereby experiencing it as more intense.

Britt shared her perspective on self-tracking her pain: "The problem with self-tracking is that there is no accurate way to express the experience of chronic pain. [This is] well known in the patient community, but there isn't a language to actively discuss it with your doctor. From my experience, I've learned to tweak the numbers in their pain assessment scales [to get] the treatment that I need..."

After realizing that the typical pain scale was not helping patients like Britt, her rheumatologist changed the pain scale poster in his office a few years ago. The new one had the same number-rating scale and miserable facial expressions but now had descriptions under each face of how that level of pain affects one's daily activities. Breakthrough! Britt had an *aha* moment! For the first time, she realized that the level of pain that interferes with concentration is considered a 6 out of

10, but more severe pain that interferes with basic needs (like not being able to shower or eat) is more like an 8 out of 10. Using this new scale, she revised her records of adaptation to suffering that spanned over two decades to something more objective, like what a person in pain can and cannot do. As Britt recalibrated to terms of functionality, she was better able to communicate her level of pain with her rheumatologist—and get better treatment. In the end, it was not self-tracking alone, but also the more accurate scale that made the scale an effective tool for Britt's pain management design.

Enthusiastic to learn how pain was functionally impacting her life, Britt then committed herself to a hardcore self-tracking experiment. She created a massive spreadsheet and planned to track each day like a true scientist—and behavior designer! She started strong: recording her meds, her mood, her diet, her activity level, her sleep, everything she could possibly think of that impacts pain. She wrote down the days when she had to take pain medicine just to get out of bed. When it seemed like too much to take a shower, she looked at the earlier data to see what could have triggered this surge of pain. Surprisingly, although she started out passionate and motivated about her self-tracking, she quickly abandoned the experiment within the first two weeks. Why would a tenacious designer like Britt not stick with collecting the vital data she needed to optimize her health?

This is a little known secret as to why self-tracking tools, apps, and wearables fail to produce long-term behavior change. Many people assume, like Britt, that if they only knew what was going on with their body and habits, they could succeed. And, yes, if we were robots using logic and rational calculations, we could use our behavior data to fix errors and optimize performance. But we have feelings. And self-tracking can be a mirror that is often too painful to look into!

"It was depressing," Britt said, "to never see improvement." On a scale of 1 to 10, she never dipped below a 7. The medication wasn't working; nothing else seemed to work either. She earnestly had wanted to see what helped but, here she was, staring at the data showing that nothing did.

To make matters worse, self-tracking made her focus her attention on the pain minute by minute, increasing her awareness—and therefore her experience—of it! Whatever we pay attention to becomes our reality. Numerous experiments have shown that if we are told to anticipate pain, our experience of it is much worse than if we are not told to expect it.[45] Therefore, focusing on her pain was trumping all the adaptive strategies Britt had mastered for ignoring pain so she could get through her day. Counterintuitively, the self-tracking was enhancing her pain experience, letting it define and control her, while disarming all the self-protective mechanisms she normally used to beat it. The tracking was focused on something so negative that it generated negative feelings. And, as we know, where emotion goes, behavior follows—even the amazingly strong Britt had to quit and regroup.

BEING A SELF-TRACKER

Self-tracking is an essential tool we need as designers. We need it to expose the unconscious patterns of our fast brain and help us sustain our slow-brain attention so that we can change our behavior. Tracking patterns in our behavior is how we figure out what is wrong, why we are doing what we do, and how our designs are working for us—or not. It is a key component of the feedback loop we need to iterate on our design and close in on what works. We need to know if we are getting warmer—or colder.

But, as we saw in Britt's story, self-tracking can be a double-edged sword. On the one hand, Britt found a self-tracking tool that better communicated her experience in objective terms that could help her doctors codesign better treatments with her. On the other hand, when Britt's self-tracking immersed her in the conscious awareness of pain, she unearthed a level of suffering she could normally suppress by focusing her attention elsewhere. We can see that self-tracking can be simultaneously enlightening to the underlying patterns that keep us in a behavioral rut, but it can also be an emotional land mine, full of frustration, disappointment, or even shame. This can trigger our natural tendency to look away—to avoid what is hard to look at in ourselves.

I have learned this from my first-hand experience. A few years ago, I was directing a weight management study that involved my team sending hundreds of digital scales to participants so we could collect their progress accurately as they went through the program. Curious about the effect this would have on them, I bought my own supercool digital scale that was also social media enabled.

Around the same time, I read a *New York Times* health article by a woman who had lost weight by tweeting her daily weight on Twitter. Having just opened a Twitter account myself and not really knowing how to use it, I decided that I would tweet my weight from my new digital scale to best understand what the people in my study were going through. The scale arrived, the setup was supereasy, and I was live, tweeting with my first weigh-in. And for a while, everything was great.

Until it wasn't.

First, there was my coworker who found me on Twitter. Being the cool guy he is, he tweeted all kinds of helpful commentary about wellness and exercise, while I tweeted out "Kyra's weight today is 140 lbs., BMI 24.2." But I just sucked it up—he was cooler than me—Twitter was not going to change that. But then, Twitter upped the ante. My ex-boyfriend started to follow me. Shortly thereafter, I started to gain some middle-aged woman weight. (If you are a middle-aged woman reading this, I know that you know that I know that you know. *smile) At first I thought, *OK, I can handle this. It will be good to overcome my ego.* But then I hit the magic number, one I didn't want tweeted out—but, of course, it immediately went out—just by my stepping on the scale. My scale had betrayed me, and Twitter had publicly exposed me (albeit to a measly public of 100 followers)! I immediately was like, "Shut it down, people, shut it down!"

I wish I could tell you there is a substitute for self-tracking. But the cold, hard truth is that tracking your data and using that self-knowledge is the fastest way to change your behavior—if you can stand it emotionally. So, how can we work with self-tracking in ways that do not make us want to crawl into the fetal position? There are a couple of safe self-tracking practices we can use.

GENTLE, SAFE, SELF-TRACKING

The first way to self-track safely is to track what you love to do and experience. Tracking your levels of enjoyment while trying new behaviors is always going to be good news. I'm reminded of a married couple I worked with who were trying to get more exercise in their lives. They both realized that they needed to be more active, so they tried to walk together. But he quit, and she was frustrated with him, thinking he did not have enough motivation. "I can't motivate the both of us," she lamented. They had tracked how often each of them walked, not what they enjoyed about their walks. In interviewing them about their walking patterns, I asked them separately about what they each liked. She enjoyed walking around the track because she liked being able to count the mile markers and measure her progress during each walk. That's great! But then I heard his side of the story. The husband's preference was all about exploring. He was willing to walk a long distance, but he loved to see new sights each time. Taking a hike or meandering through the farmers market was ideal—everything was new and interesting. When he suggested that they go for a wandering walk, it didn't feel like exercise to her. When she suggested they hit the track, it felt boring and redundant to him. But they did not track how their self-tracking preferences were killing their exercise together. As an outsider, I was able to identify this pattern that, like that fish in water, they didn't see yet. As a result of designing around what each of them enjoyed, we were able to create a plan that met both of their needs and brought them back together to support each other.

Another way to self-track without hurting yourself is not to do it alone. The Weight Watchers model is a good example of how social support can help people face the tedium and emotional land mines of self-tracking. Let's face it: counting calories is never an exercise in joy! It is like inching toward failure, bite by bite. The more you count, the more disheartening it gets. Instead of focusing on healthy eating, we can't help but focus on deprivation—what we cannot have, that we are "done eating for the day." And, of course, should we overshoot and eat too much, we just stepped in a giant cow patty of shame!

The Weight Watchers program has evolved to deal with the inherent negatives of calorie counting. First, it offers group support. Second, it sets the expectation that you gain and lose weight (thereby reducing self-judgment). Finally, it focuses on coaching and tracking technology that makes it more pleasant to track calories, and sprinkles the process with encouragement from real people who have been there. Smart design.

I am not advocating for Weight Watchers in particular because I believe different methods work for different people. What I am saying is this: when you have to track anything that may be remotely emotionally difficult, don't do it alone. Support in groups has been proven to be lifesaving. Long ago, many doctors thought that social support groups were just touchy-feely. But now we know that social support improves quality of life and, sometimes, even survival of cancer, for example. Maybe that is one tweak to Britt's design that could have helped—although she was brave enough to track her pain and then share it honestly with her Twitter and blog audience, perhaps she needed another person (or more) to do it with her. We humans are stronger together than we ever are alone.

A final approach to self-tracking that is not harmful is something called beginner's mind. This is a Buddhist concept of holding the mindset of a novice—someone who is just starting and is therefore open, curious, and without blame. This means not "should-ing" on yourself. Should-ing is the exact opposite of being a beginner—with should-ing you are holding yourself accountable for things you think you should do or should already know better. Instead, with beginner's mind, if your weight goes up, or you scream at the kids again, there is a curiosity instead of self-judgment, an interest in how to improve rather than disappointment that you did not do it right. With beginner's mind, self-tracking is a stream of helpful information instead of a feedback loop of failure. To practice this, you might say a mantra to yourself that releases you from self-judgment like, *I am just a student of all that is happening, I am learning, I don't have to already know anything.*

DEEP TRACKING

I mentioned earlier that tracking our own behavior exposes insights that are normally psychologically hidden to us. But even more than tracking our actual behaviors—what we do and say—is tracking the thoughts and emotions that drive our behaviors. Knowing what fuels our behaviors at the deepest level—*why* we do what we do—is especially powerful for understanding and then being able to change what we do.

We all have habitual thought and emotional patterns. We unconsciously experience these strong neural networks as *Me*. We may even claim them as our temperament or our personality, when in fact they are just fabricated, usually in childhood, to protect or promote our sense of self. In fact, our tendency to think and feel a particular way can be so strongly conditioned and wired that we cannot see it as the creator and driver of our behavior—we just see the output of our actions. It is like we are watching the output of our inner "thought engine," like watching exhaust pour out of a tailpipe— spitting out what we do and what we say—and then claiming, "Hey, that's me!"

The first time I ever experienced this for myself absolutely blew my mind. I had signed up for a beginner's meditation class with my teacher, Sylvia. The class was on negative emotions. She started out with a small lecture describing how our minds are constantly and endlessly streaming thoughts, and that these thoughts are primarily negative in their commentary. Emotions, she said, could be triggered spontaneously by a series of thoughts that intensified. "Think of an emotion as a 'thought storm,' she said. Then she had us close our eyes and simply watch what was happening with our thoughts, instructing us to notice how many there were and what they were saying. *Easy enough*, I thought, and followed the instructions to close my eyes. She rang a bell to start the meditation.

I can describe the experience as opening the door to a loud party. As soon as I closed my eyes, I saw and heard my own thoughts as a cacophony of nonstop chatter. I noticed how self-critical many of my thoughts were: *Why am I doing this? OK, try to stop thinking. You're failing! Stop blinking your eyes so much, you don't look relaxed. Gawd, when is this going to be over?* Once she rang the bell to stop the meditation, I opened my eyes to realize that I was indeed living at the end of a tailpipe, now having witnessed the engine.

So what, you might ask? Why should we have to

bother with the unconscious machinations of our brain and track them ever so carefully?

In self-tracking, it's not only what you do that matters, it's why. Remember that our fast brain is driving most of our behaviors—and decisions—before our conscious slow brain realizes it. In fact, brain studies have detected through fMRI that we actually make decisions seconds before we consciously know what we have chosen to do.[46] We are like a country dog chasing behind our fast-brain car, zooming down the road before our slow brain can change our course. This means that we are not operating of our own free will. Ahem! We are not living our birthright of free will! Rather, we are helplessly and habitually repeating over and over thoughts and actions that may not be in our best interest. We are not free. And that is where the deeper tracking of our thoughts and emotions helps us—so we can be free.

Remember the implicit memory system? That's the built-in self-tracking system we already have—except we do not have conscious access to the data and patterns that it holds. As a result, we are prone to shifting our behavior according to its hidden conclusions. Just like the husband who did not know why he stopped walking with his wife until he became aware of his emotional need to explore on walks, if we track the emotions and thoughts that are underneath what we do, we will know how to design a fix for them. Deep tracking makes you a better designer. The deeper the insights that drive your behavior design, the longer your design will last and the more effective it will be.

So how do we track deep, silent, and fast patterns like those of our thoughts and emotions? This is where awareness practices come in. Awareness practices like meditation, journaling, contemplation, yoga, and others help us stabilize our attention. Stabilized attention, in turn, enables us to see the underlying patterns of our behavior—like watching a hummingbird fly in slow motion so we can see the movement of each wing instead of the blur we would see in real time.

When we take the time to practice awareness using whatever methods work for us, it is like lowering the water level around an iceberg—we can see more of the iceberg. It is simple. If we are always distracted and letting our fast brain and implicit memory just react spastically to life, we will be stuck in repeating behaviors that may forever obscure the best version of ourselves. But if we invest in building our awareness, slowing down to examine what our underlying thoughts and emotions are, we can use this information to inspire a better design to change our behavior.

And really, this is about spending time to save time. If we put off building awareness and instead leave our implicit memory to take charge of solving our problems and running our behaviors, it will take a very long time and lots of suffering to finally realize that what we are doing is not working. The implicit memory takes years to bubble up to the surface to reveal that we keep picking the same unhealthy relationships, that we are stifled in our workplace, or that our heart's desire is to be an artist. Dedicating our time to awareness practice and seeing how our inner mind operates catalyzes our understanding and saves us from a life of futile struggle. It's your choice: long, frustrating suffering path or shorter, clearer self-aware path.

I remember the first time I really understood the value of awareness practice. I had always considered myself a very aware person. Since childhood, parents and teachers praised me about how observant I was.

During medical school, I worked closely with another classmate to start a nonprofit for at-risk teens. She and I would spend hours and days together nonstop. Inevitably, we would disagree about how something should be done or who should do what. In our arguments, I always felt I had an advantage because whereas she was very intelligent, she was not that aware, and I could sway her to my point of view. That was, until she started meditating.

One day, we started into another disagreement, debating over something so insignificant I cannot remember it now. What I do remember is that in the middle of our discourse, I said something in an effort to get her on my side, and she stopped me right in my tracks. "You're just saying that so that I will go along with you!" she corrected. I was amazed—she could see right through me—and I did not even know I was doing that until she pointed it out! Her ability to see both of our underlying thoughts and emotions had been heightened by her meditation practice. Being the competitive person I was, I immediately started to meditate (signing up for the class with Sylvia, who I described earlier).

Not the best of motivations to start, I know. My ego wishes I could impress you with a story of my enlightened start in meditation, but that is not who I was at the time. And that's really the point. I have since matured because of the insights I obtained through meditation, iterating and upgrading my behavior into the better, healthier, and more honest person that I am today. That is what meditation and other awareness practices offer for anyone who puts in the time to practice.

SELF-TRACKING AS ATTENTION

Recall from our last chapter that long-term behavior change is merely a function of our stable, repetitive attention. The whole point of self-tracking is to create a vehicle for sustained attention so that we gain awareness, which, in turn, enables us to design for a better life. Self-tracking is feeding the baby wolf that we're trying to raise.

But it's hard to pay attention to one thing for very long—especially in our fast-paced world, where we are overstimulated by smartphones, e-mails, and media most of the time. Self-tracking, by its very nature, can be intensive and requires a lot of attention (and, as we learned, stimulates emotion). Think of taking the long-term view here.

Even professional athletes have rest days or an off-season. In part, this reflects the organic human need for seasonal focus. We are built for intensive activity then rest periods. Many workplaces sponsor team competitions to encourage their employees to get healthy. The typical season for these competitions is 16 weeks—no one can compete year-round and maintain their interest in the same activity without variety. This is the best way to design your self-tracking as well.

Seasonal self-tracking works because our brain pays attention to contrast. Consider a basic experiment in sensory science that demonstrates the brain's heightened responsiveness to contrast through a laboratory task called an oddball task.[47] In effect, study participants doing an oddball task are presented with a string of stimuli that are identical; it could be the same image, the same sound, or the same word. Imagine hearing *ping... ping... ping... ping... ping....* But then an oddball sound comes along. When the brain hears *ping... ping... pong*, its activity surges in a very specific way on the *pong*.

There is a well-characterized brain waveform called the P300, so named because it is a positive spike of electricity (*P* stands for *positive*) that happens with a regular time stamp, 300 milliseconds after the odd stimulus— the *pong* in this case. There are some differences in the height of the P300 peak between visual and auditory stimuli, and even this P300 oddball response wave starts to adapt (get weaker) over time with repetition of the same image or same sound. But the P300 always persists, showing us that the brain is continually on the lookout for what is new and different. It craves novel stimulation.

This means that we absolutely will get bored of self-tracking. I don't care how much you love your shiny new fitness wearable thingamajig that you got for Christmas, the data shows that by summer you're likely over it. Therefore, plan for this boredom. When we design a way to track our behavior patterns, we must also expect that our design of self-tracking will expire. Having a self-tracking active season and an off-season helps us get our own attention back and takes advantage of our tendency to need contrast.

WEARABLES

One group dedicated to the art and science of self-tracking is the Quantified Self. Started by Gary Wolf and Kevin Kelly, this association of users and makers of self-tracking tools has produced a movement through meetings, conferences, and forums. Having been to several meetings of this group, I am always impressed by the passion and intelligence applied to the scientific method of self-tracking. By definition, the self-tracker archetype tends to be detail-oriented, methodical, and rigorous—basically, precision geeks. And in my experience working with healthcare data at the millions-of-people level, only about 5 percent of the general population tends to be true, quantified self-trackers—apparently the other 95 percent prefer to "guestimate." But our brains are terrible at estimating such data, which is why we grossly overestimate how many calories we burn during exercise and underestimate the number of calories we eat. Our brains tell us, *hey, I got this, no problem. I am counting everything,* when in reality it is like asking a four-year-old child to count to 100 without getting distracted.

Recently, health enthusiasts have pointed to the wearable device market as a way for self-tracking to hit the masses. The advent of HealthKit by Apple offers a nod to the possibility of large-scale self-tracking through integrating data from any number of wristbands, chest bands, stickers, ear buds, or clip-on pedometers. Technologists are creating ways for us to measure just about everything we do using a device. Many are hopeful that the convenience of these devices will make it easier to self-track. And that part may be true. But remember my experience with the digital scale.

Wearables, as they are known, can unintentionally create emotional backlash, just like I experienced when tweeting my weight or what Britt experienced tracking her pain. They can have unexpected social implications like that experienced by a professional athlete I know who wore an activity tracking wristband only to be teased by her former teammates. They incredulously said, "You *need* one of those?" In that high-motivation and high-performance subculture, such a device indicates you need help remembering to work out. And how about the rest of us? Once our wearable gadget tells us a story we don't want to hear, like our progress is declining or stagnating, guess what? We don't use it anymore.

Whether on our wrist, belt, shoe, ear, or inside our mobile app, wearables offer the same emotional mirrors of any self-tracking method. We course through a relationship with them that has several predictable phases. First, wearables are like shiny new toys; they are fascinating and we check them often. The contrast and novelty gets our attention. After a while, however, we may not match up to our ambitious, fixed goals (remember the win-loss psychology of goal-setting) and the habenula counts it against us. Or, alternatively, we notice that our data doesn't change a whole lot day-to-day, week-to-week, so without the contrast, we get bored. Either way, as a consequence we finally move into the last phase, where we start to be inconsistent. Remember that inconsistent behaviors indicate a design is expiring. We may forget to put the wearable back on after showering or after recharging it. If it is an app, we may not even "see" it on our screen anymore. Finally, our attention has waned. Interest in the wearable has expired. We must move on and figure out a new way to get our own attention back and create meaningful feedback into our behavior that is helpful and enjoyable.

As far as I can tell, there are two ways to prolong the use of wearables. The first strategy is to have an active season that requires the wearable as a tool—like using it to train for a race or event—and an off-season. This also includes changing devices for contrast if you can.

The second strategy is to use a wearable as a social currency, like in a group competition. So far, however, this has been fraught with cheating, like the guy I sat next to at Starbucks who was just sitting there shaking his wristband to get points because he said his friend tied his wristband to his dog.

The third strategy is to change your emotional expectations of the wearable. Most people (unconsciously) think of a wearable as a goal-setting and behavior-changing device. This causes them to have emotions like disappointment, frustration, and disillusionment when the device does not change their behavior. But what if we think of a wearable as a self-tracking device—providing big-picture information only? We can then have a response somewhat similar to beginner's mind and just be curious about the process of changing our behavior. We focus on designing the change in our behavior from the feedback data we receive from the device, and we no longer expect the data to magically change our behavior. We see the device as an enabler to iterate. By holding a beginner's mindset around what we are seeing, we can also avoid any negative emotional traps that would cause us to stop.

FEEDBACK LOOP

In behavior design, the concept of a feedback loop is very important. It is the way that you close in on yourself. The whole point of self-tracking is to build a feedback loop that allows you to see patterns in the shortest amount of time possible. Without gathering data on your own behavior, you could still catch yourself, you could still see the wrestling match between fast brain and slow brain, but it will take much longer. It might take years or, even worse, it might never happen. Sadly, you might never see it and always live in the gap between what you say you want and what you actually do. However, if you boldly start to track your behavior and the deeper thoughts and emotions that drive it, you can generate insights to fuel design thinking that changes behavior.

The longer you self-track a behavior, the shorter the time lapse between habitually doing the undesired old behavior with your fast brain and realizing it with your slow brain. For instance, it may be the difference between regretting a food binge hours afterward once you are feeling bloated and icky and realizing during the binge, even as you put the food in your mouth, that you don't want to be doing this. As the time lapse shrinks, you approach an opportune moment of overlap between awareness, self-tracking, and behavior, and only until these converge do you have any real free will to choose a different behavior.

As we did when we started this chapter with the story of the heroic Britt, we have to acknowledge that self-tracking is not for the faint of heart. Rather, it can be an emotional minefield. Know what to bring along with you for the journey. Yes. Self-compassion. You are bravely looking under the hood—at the engine behind all that you do. Frankly, this is something that most people are afraid to do. Avoidance, addiction, illogic, and confusion all lurk there. But so do insights, freedom from the past, and your best self!

PUTTING IT INTO PRACTICE

At the heart of everything that we're learning here is how to design our behavior. By its very nature, design requires iteration—small steps and tweaks, like Britt's tinkering. To be more effective in our tinkering and to save time in the long run, we are wise to work with the deepest insights we can. Self-tracking fosters insight, making us better designers. However, the brain can pose obstacles to self-tracking—like negative thoughts and emotions in response to the disappointing data we are seeing about ourselves. It is super important, therefore, to practice self-compassion and beginner's mind as a way to get to the bottom of what we do—and why—so we can design for a better way.

Self-Tracking

Here are a few questions to help you incorporate self-tracking into your approach to behavior change:

For the behavior you want to change, what pattern would you want to self-track to gain insights or create a feedback loop?

_____

_____

_____

Is there anything unpleasant about tracking that pattern?

_____

_____

_____

Can you think of a different pattern, such as something you find more pleasant or even pleasurable to track? Something that you could substitute?

_____

_____

_____

What is probably going to bore you about tracking this pattern?

_____

_____

_____

How can you use it off-season, make it social, or use a beginner's mind to keep it fresh?

_____

How would you work the insights from this self-tracking feedback into a design?

How would what you learn from the self-tracking patterns help you tinker and iterate on your design?

Notes

8

future self, past self— BFFs or frenemies?

At the center of your being you have the answer;
you know who you are,
and you know what you want.

—Lao Tzu

People make plans all the time that they do not follow. Just as a fashion design team spends its time reviewing the latest color trends, at my company, engagedIN, we spend our time discussing behavior design—why people do what they do and how they can do what they truly wish to do.

On one particular week, our team meeting was at a health club because we wanted to learn more about workout patterns. We sat in the club restaurant, chatting about our own personal workout routines over some appetizers. We have a variety of folks on our team: a couple of former elite athletes who played professionally or in college, others who played high school team sports, and a few like me, who grew up doing a variety of individual gym workouts and classes. Each person described their fitness approach and how they got themselves to do it in terms of designing their behavior. One of our designers, Cynthia, spoke first.

"I start on Sunday night, planning each workout for the coming week. I plan which exercises I will do on what day, how hard I will work, and how long I will go," she described.

We were all impressed and asked her how she can be so organized and structured.

She answered, "I just don't want to waste my time. For me, it is all about being efficient. When I am at the gym, I want to follow my plan exactly—no chitchat, no phone, no distractions. I arrive, I work hard, and I go home. It's not a social thing."

The whole table was in awe of her freakish self-discipline. We grilled her for more details about her design, all the while murmuring to ourselves in disbelief. Maybe you have guessed by now that she was a professional athlete.

"Wow, I can't even imagine following such a rigid plan!" I said, "How do you not rebel against yourself?"

Cynthia smiled kindly. "Yeah, that's a good question," she pondered, "I guess I feel like I would be letting myself down."

Another designer on our team rang in.

"That's interesting because I think I am the exact opposite," Wyatt started, "Since the baby was born, I haven't had time for hockey, so I have been going to the gym whenever I can fit it in."

"Do you plan ahead at all?" asked another designer.

"You know, I think it just comes to me, like 'oh, it's been awhile, maybe I should work out tonight' and I just do it spontaneously," he recalled. "But I don't go very often and it's really inconsistent when I do. I have tried to plan ahead, but when the time comes, I'm too busy or something comes up with the baby and I bail."

Contrast these two approaches with that of another designer: me.

"When I was younger, working out was easy, fun, and rewarding: work hard, get results! But what I have noticed is that as I get older, working out hurt more, and it took more to get the same results. After a while, I couldn't make myself work hard enough at the gym. So I tried yoga, boot camp, and barre classes—because I needed to be surrounded by other people who were pushing themselves, so I would push myself too. I also need to buy individual classes instead of the monthly subscription because if I don't use them, I still own them. I find it depressing to pay for a month of unlimited classes, not use them because I am traveling or whatever, then feel like I overpaid," I confessed.

As others shared their workout routines, a theme emerged. Each of us, whether Cynthia's highly regimented plans or Wyatt's loosey-goosey impulsive style or my class-by-class commitment, had designed something for our future self—the one who had to carry out the plan. And that future self had a specific relationship with the past self who had designed and obligated them to carry out that plan. In Cynthia's case, it seemed she had the healthiest relationship between her future self and her past self—they were like besties! Her future self was so kind and thoughtful; she did not want to let her past self down. Contrast that to Wyatt, whose future self would probably say something like, "oh, sorry, something just came up." Or my own future self who may want to say to my past self, "You spent *what* on unlimited classes? Why did you think that was a good deal? You know I had a lot of travel this month—when exactly was I going to take those classes?"

In each case, you can see the individual's self-image of *Me* and *Not Me* in between the lines, right? Cynthia's "I'm a highly trained athlete, I'm not a time waster." Wyatt's "I'm spontaneous, I'm not a planner." My "I'm busy, I cannot be obligated." As we covered earlier, it's the underlying self-image that determines what we will and will not do. And, more specifically, it's the self-image of the future self that is going to matter when the time comes.

YOUR RELATIONSHIP WITH YOUR FUTURE SELF

Now that we can see more clearly that we are designing for our future self, what matters most is the "relationship" between our past and future selves. How well do these two get along? What is their dynamic? Are they helping each other out? Is your past self setting up your future self to fail with harsh and insensitive plans and designs? Is your future self reacting with passive-aggressive behavior, rebelling like a teenager or sabotaging all the designs meant to engage her?

Recently, my mother illustrated a perfect example of this. She said I could share it with you because she has a most wonderful sense of humor about her own behavior. Admittedly, having a daughter who designs behavior for a living is kind of like having a comedian in the family—you know that your story will be worked into the act at some point. (Plus, my family does not make me sign nondisclosure agreements like my clients do!) Here's how it goes.

It's a few months until my wedding in Kauai and my mother is trying to drop a few pounds. She tries a bunch of her old favorite strategies: a cabbage "diet" soup, eating smaller portions, cutting out soda. But she is not seeing any results—either because her habenula is rising up against these old, expired designs, or her body is just older and it responds differently than it used to. On top of that, she is weighing herself daily, and when she gains even 1 pound, which she refuses to believe is within the limits of normal daily fluctuation of water weight, she gets discouraged. When she gets discouraged, her unconscious fast brain says, *Screw this! If I'm going down, I'm going down in flames!* and she proceeds to binge until she is engorged like a swollen tick. She also has a lifelong addiction to eating popcorn in front of home improvement shows at night—there are worse addictions. Oh, and she absolutely hates to exercise. So, that's my mom.

We talk often by phone because she still lives in Oklahoma. I have been listening to her chronicles of dieting, not wanting to interfere because I didn't want to encourage dieting. Plus you know how families are; you could be a Nobel laureate in your field and your family still would not listen to your advice. Finally, after listening to her struggle for weeks, I could not watch my mother struggle anymore, so I started to help her design her behavior.

And it worked! My mom started to make progress. She loved the idea that she was designing her healthy behaviors—it put her in the driver's seat, not me. She would text (yes, text!) me her small successes and ask me questions about labels while grocery shopping. She consulted with her best girlfriend, Lu, who has diabetes and knows a lot about low-carb eating. My mom was on fire!

But she had an Achilles' heel: microwave popcorn. She went through all the distinct stages of grief with the realization that popcorn was a carb-o-licious snack. First, she denied that popcorn was not healthy. Then she was angry and depressed that it was high carb. Then she started to bargain with herself—eating one bag, then two, then infinity. She called me once she saw her addiction in full swing to vent her frustration.

"Mom, why don't you get those mini-bags of popcorn? That way, you will have a whole minute while it pops in the microwave for your slow brain to catch up with what your fast brain is habitually doing, but you will limit the damage your fast brain can do because you'll pop less corn." (Notice the harm reduction in the suggested design.)

She thought that was a great design, we hung up, and a week went by. Then she called again.

"I am so depressed about the popcorn. I can't enjoy my shows without it, but if I have it I feel so guilty!"

"Mom, remember that you can have popcorn—we designed for that. Did you buy the mini-bags?"

"Well, I tried to, but when I read the box, it said they had a lot of calories and carbs for each mini-bag, and they were more expensive per ounce. So I bought the large bags thinking I would divide the larger bag into three smaller sandwich bags and eat one per day. But that lasted for about two days before I just ended up eating the whole big bag."

Slightly frustrated but feeling compassion, I inquired.

"Mom, what happened? I thought we agreed you would buy the mini-bags!"

"Yes, but the mini-bags had so many carbs I didn't want to eat that many."

"But mom," I argued, "I'm pretty sure the mini-bags have fewer carbs than that whole big bag you ended up eating!"

She laughed hard, "Yeah, I guess that's true."

"Mom," I said, "You have to design for what your future self will actually do, not what you hope she will do. It's like your future self didn't like what your past self had created for her—whether it was too restrictive or unpleasant—and so it rebelled."

"Yes, yes, that's exactly what happened! OK, I am going to go get the mini-bags!"

The relationship my mother had with her popcorn-craving future self was dysfunctional. It was like her past self was a harsh captor, imposing all kinds of deprivation and shame on her future self. Her future self, in turn, was breaking out of "the pen" and running free and rampant—eating all the popcorn it wanted in its path. My mom and I actually started talking about her future self in this humorous way, calling it Future

Markie (my mom's first name). We spoke of her behavior designs in terms of whether Future Markie would like them or would rebel. When she saw herself break out of the pen, so to speak, we would talk about what kinds of designs would make Future Markie content so she wouldn't want to break out of the pen, but would feel comfortable and happy there. We have had a lot of fun and laughs with it.

She recently texted me: "Got up and weight was great. Have lost 10 pounds in total."

And that's really the point: remember to be a compassionate designer. No need to inflict big, hairy, audacious plans for your future self to carry out. No need to suck the joy out of life just to make yourself healthier or to reach your ideal goal. We gravitate toward what makes us feel smart and appreciated—what makes us feel seen and heard. That which makes us feel fabulous. In contrast, we run from what makes us feel less capable and unappreciated—even when that is our past self.

A great designer has compassion for the person that they're designing for—and you are your own client. When you wake up to the 5:00 a.m. alarm that your past self set, show up to the awkward date it arranged, stay up late trying to complete the unrealistic to-do list it set for you, have compassion. Speak to your past self with kindness. This attitude helps the past and future selves get along, just like a loving partnership.

Basically, if your future self is breaking out of the pen and you are not following through on your plans, it is a symptom of the dysfunction in the design relationship with yourself. Something is wrong. As we covered already, the design may be too hard. It also may be too soft—like letting your future self resort to bad habits, like eating the whole popcorn bag. Both can be true. Your past self can be unfair and your future self can be lazy and naughty. And when either of these arise, a fundamental breakdown in your own self-trust occurs, which can do a lot of damage to your psyche.

BUILDING SELF-TRUST

After I finished medical school, I started and ran an organization for incarcerated urban youth that focused on behavior change. Most of the youth in our program were repeat offenders. A product of the violence and crime in their neighborhoods, these young people resorted to behavior that was normal for their environment but that they knew deep down was wrong.

Whenever I would speak to one of them while they were locked up, they would soberly and remorsefully tell me their true desires—the vast majority secretly wanted to leave their gang and crime forever. This, of course, was their slow-brain, logical self. But over and over again, once they got out and had their freedom again, they ran back to the *Me* that they knew so well. It never ceased to amaze me how sincere they were when they had time, and the basic food, shelter, and clothing of juvenile detention (notice this put them higher on Maslow's hierarchy) to reflect on their true experience of street life and their true desires for themselves. It also never ceased to amaze me how quickly they would turn to the streets and gangs once they were released—a testament to how powerful an influence environment is for all of us.

One conversation I had with a 16-year-old youth stood out to me as a lesson in self-trust. I was visiting him while he was incarcerated. He was about to finish an 11-month sentence for assault, and we were discussing his plans post release.

"I want to go back to school," he told me. "I've been learning how to read while up in here and I'm thinking I could do well in school when I get out."

"Of course, you can, Dante, you are obviously super smart." He lit up at the rare compliment and positive image of himself.

"But," he paused, "on the outside, none of my friends goes to school so I started not to go."

"What do you mean?"

"I mean, we be smoking weed and all and then... I don't wanna do nothing," he hesitated to search for my reaction.

"So, you don't trust yourself not to smoke weed and instead make it to school?" I asked.

"Yeah! I really wanna do better, but when it comes up, I don't," he said with a somber tone.

Based on this conversation, our organization set up a paid internship program through which we rewarded youth to work on their own follow through as if it were their job, so they could build self-trust little by little.

I have noticed that self-trust or lack thereof is the deciding factor in whether we succeed or fail, whether we keep trying or quit. I see this with individuals. I also see this with confident teams who come from behind to beat the team that held the lead most of the game—they trust themselves. It has nothing to do with the potential of the person or the team. As a nod to chapter 5, it also has nothing to do with having motivation. Self-trust has to do with how often you have experienced successfully showing up for yourself (or your team) and the confidence that builds in you. It is a measure of the integrity you have with yourself between what you say and what you do.

In my field of health and wellness, there is a lot of talk about self-efficacy. People who score high on self-efficacy measures are more confident in their ability to advocate for themselves, to complete goals, and to generally succeed.[48] They have better outcomes, save more on health expenses, and are generally happier.

But I would argue that self-efficacy is not just self-esteem (thinking well of yourself). Rather, I think it is a result of many cycles of building self-trust, where you see your future self fulfill what your past self had designed for it. I think self-efficacy is an outcome of self-trust—knowing that you will not let yourself down.

Why is this an important distinction? Because even if I am convinced that self-efficacy is the key to success, I don't know how to build or design for self-efficacy. It is too abstract. It is not actionable or designable. Where does it come from? It seems to magically exist or not. How does it arise? Is it only for people with good childhoods or from loving, supportive, two-parent households? How is it different from self-esteem?

But building self-trust is a cleaner target. It gives me a clue about what I am designing for. Focused on self-trust, I know that I have to rein in my overambitious past self who will overcommit my future self. I also know that I must build a more appealing, less harmful pen for my sometimes lazy, sometimes rebellious future self. I know that I need self-compassionate language to build the relationship between the two and to even forgive myself when I get it wrong. And I know that my self-trust likely leads to self-confidence and self-efficacy.

A lot of the same concepts that we covered when learning about self-tracking in the last chapter apply here as well. For instance, when you design for getting (and refreshing) your own attention, it is none other than your future self's attention you are grabbing. When your future self starts to ignore the things your past self designed for it, this is merely an indicator that the design is either boring or incomplete (i.e., there's a hole in the fence and your future self broke out of the pen). The loss of attention means your past self might have to liven things up a bit and add some novelty, surprise, delight, reward, or meaning (like pulling ideas from quadrant 1 or 3 in the motivation-emotion 2×2 table).

THE ASPIRATIONAL FUTURE SELF

Have you ever bought something that you never used? Simply put, that item was a gift from your past self to your future self. It was an aspirational purchase, in hopes that your future self would take up yoga, ride a stationary bike at home, or eventually fit into those designer jeans one size too small (Hey, they were on sale!). But in the end, the yoga mat sits in the closet, the stationary bike becomes a laundry hanger, and the jeans move to the bottom of the drawer for a while before they eventually are donated to charity in defeat. The advertising industry knows this phenomenon of our buying behavior all too well—creating aspirational ads for absolutely everything we could want—or rather, everything our past self could hope for.

Instead, let's be realistic.

Remember in chapter 5 we saw that our motivations are either stable or unstable. When our future self does not follow through with what the past self designed for it, then the design was built on shaky ground: an unstable motivation. Therefore, being realistic means that we ask ourselves one question when we are designing for our future self: Is my future self going to have the same motivation I have right now, or will the motivation be unstable or dominated by other motivations by that time?

Likewise, when we need to clear out the unused things that our past self bought for us, like the yoga mat, the bike, or the jeans, we can be honest with ourselves and donate them. Letting go of our past self's aspirational purchases and commitments that do not work for us helps build self-trust. Our future self is being honest with our past self. By shedding these reminders of wasted time and money, we can be free of shame for not following through or guilt for not doing what we said we would. Then we are only doing what we are stably motivated and ready to do—and meanwhile buying and using only what we need.

DESIGNING INCENTIVES

You may think, *OK, if I as my past self am trying to entice my future self to do something I really want, why don't I just create an incentive?* And you would be right. But most people do not use incentives correctly and do not realize that misusing incentives leads them farther away from their vision. Here's an example:

A well-meaning friend of mine wanted her 13-year-old son to feel better about himself because he was struggling in school. He did not have motivation for school and avoided every aspect of it: homework, activities, and, often, even attending class. She was recently divorced so she felt that her son was missing his dad, in particular having a male role model around to do guy things with. She felt helpless to fill this role. But when his dad left, he left behind a remnant of manhood in the garage: his woodworking bench and a few tools.

Her son started to tinker with his dad's tools, perhaps to touch the memory of having him in the house. He made a few simple things at first, a doorknob, a longbow for his archery kit. It turned out he was extraordinarily talented, almost prodigious, with molding and creating works of art out of wood.

My friend was so excited, and she wanted to acknowledge and encourage him. She asked him to make stuff for the house. She researched local woodworking clubs, comprised mostly of adults, and found a male role model who was willing to mentor her son. Everything looked promising—even if school was not a source of validation, she thought, certainly woodworking could be.

Then—nothing. Her son abandoned woodworking. He stopped going into the garage. No matter how much she suggested he do it again or asked him to make something else, he did not touch the equipment again.

So, what happened?

When I used to work daily with teens, especially teenage boys, I used to coach parents on incentivizing positive behaviors. One metaphor I used was the myth that if a baby bird falls out of the nest and you touch it, the parent bird will abandon it because they smell human scent (which is not actually true, but the metaphor is perfect). In other words, whenever a teenager takes up woodworking it can be really exciting for the parent, much like finding a cute, helpless baby bird on the ground. But as soon as the teen "smells" the parent's "scent" on what they care about, they abandon it. Unintentionally, the parent converts an incentive that was internal to the teen and makes it external—just by taking a position on it.

In one way incentives are simple; they fall into one of two categories: they either connect internally (aka intrinsic motivation, which is the clinical term) or externally (aka extrinsic motivation). Intrinsic motivation occurs when we act without any obvious external rewards but merely out of enjoyment, meaning, or self-satisfaction. No one tells us to do it, we just want to because it makes us feel good about ourselves. Random acts of kindness, like opening doors for others or helping someone out, are perfect examples of common human behaviors that we do for our own internal reward. Generally, incentives that tap into intrinsic motivations are emotional payoffs that are personal and private—like making an amazing piece of woodcraft without anyone knowing.

On the opposite end of the spectrum lie incentives that dock into our extrinsic motivation. These can be monetary, like a salary or payment for some performance, or any time we gain or lose materially. They can also be social, like getting compliments when we rock some outfit at our friend's cocktail party, or any time we get praise from others. Finally, they may have an emotional component, for example, when we stay up all night to finish something for work so that we avoid social disgrace the next day. That last one is a mix of social and emotional.

External incentives have their place and time. They can be effective at getting us things we would otherwise ignore, like getting an annual physical exam if we are rewarded by our employer to do so. They are also effective at getting us do something extraordinary—just look at the accomplishments by contestants on certain TV shows like *The Biggest Loser*. Those contestants would never go through all that effort and suffering were it not for the social (look, I'm on TV!), emotional (someone else cares), and possibly financial (prize money) incentives.

Many employers, seeing that external incentives work to get people to do something amazing, have emulated this by creating *Biggest Loser*-like workplace challenges. And they work for a while. But there's a catch—there is a human (resources) scent all over that baby bird! If we know our mother, boss, spouse, or any other onlooker is behind the incentive, we may abandon our baby bird.

It has been well documented that positive external incentives, aka carrots (for leading the proverbial donkey with food), can kill internal motivation.[49] Using external incentives long term is like a heroin addiction. The first few times, it creates a high. Then, as we discussed in prior chapters, it is required to feel normal. Then we build a tolerance for this type of incentive and more and more is needed to get the same results. For example, if you get paid $50 cash to do something that you really don't want to do, you'll do it the first time and maybe the second. Over time, however, you'll put a higher price tag on the task because it is not internally satisfying. Meanwhile, your intrinsic memory that has accounted for your flattening emotional experience is signaling *I got nothing*. In other words, you'll adapt to the size of the incentive, even feeling entitled to the payout because getting the $50 is now yours—it has been integrated into your self-image *Me* center. *Give me my money!* it says.

Treats, cash, and badges are all external motivators. Paychecks are as well but have a special status as a motivator because they are so tightly linked to other basic needs—survival needs like food and housing—so they are more sustainable. In all cases, positive external incentives can lead to a behavior only as long as they are there. When the incentives stop, so does the behavior.

Another popular use of external incentives is negative—aka a stick (for prodding the proverbial donkey from behind). In 2002, the Nobel Prize in economics was awarded to Drs. Daniel Kahneman and Vernon L. Smith for their work in loss economics. In short, they proved that we humans are far more sensitive to loss than we are to gain. To be exact, we are twice as sensitive to loss as we are gain. This means that we will fight tooth and nail to keep something we have, like a $20 bill, but we may give a big fat *meh* to that $40 gift card from some sales offer.

Riding on this psychological discovery, the field of behavior economics has been exploding in recent years. From the time limits of purchasing a concert ticket online to Snapchat's disappearing photos to losing out on a discount on your health insurance if you do not get your biometric screening done, the design of loss-based incentives is permeating every aspect of our world.

However, here again, negative, stick, external incentives have their limit—and that limit is rebellion from the future self (aka a psychological term called *reactance*). Recall that I recommended going easy on the future self—creating a habitat that it enjoys and a pace that creates feelings of success. At the same time, what do we do when our future self is getting distracted or just being lazy? Here is what I suggest: negative external incentives can be used as a one-time "shot in the rear" to get the future self moving on the design as long as it does not create a huge backlash. Avoid using negative external incentives that will generate shame, guilt, regret, or resentment because your future self will eventually find a way to shut it down because it feels bad, and we do not like to feel bad.

There are other ways to use incentives correctly when designing behavior. External incentives can evolve into internal incentives when repeated enough, but only if they get associated with a pleasant emotional or social experience (or give repeated relief from a negative emotion). An example would be a very shy child who gets recognition for her art piece in the 2nd grade and repeatedly throughout school. She then goes on to create a personal art studio in her college apartment and eventually becomes a full-time professional artist. What started out as external world praise eventually became integrated into her positive self-image and was internalized and adopted as *Me* for a personally satisfying career.

Another way to use incentives, according to the early research on variable rewards by Skinner,[50] is to make sure your external incentives, positive or negative, have some variety built in. This helps positive carrot incentives keep their flavor (i.e., attention from the brain) and protects negative stick incentives from creating a sore (i.e., rebellion) by poking us in the same spot over and over.

Social incentives are especially powerful for this. I credit author Nir Eyal for something he said over lunch one day: "I think social interaction is the ultimate source of variety for triggering behavior." What he means by this is that you may ignore your mobile app push notification or wearable band telling you to get more active, but if a close friend texts you to go running, you are much more likely to pay attention. Since external incentives are a form of environmental triggering, the same rules apply; the brain starts to ignore incentives that lack variability (just like the *ping... ping... ping... pong* experiment). Social rewards are the most powerful and most variable of all external incentives, so make them work for you!

And while social rewards can be powerful external incentives, the most stable and longest lasting incentive of all is internal. In fact, we only use external incentives when we do not know how to tap into our intrinsic motivation. As a rule, internal incentives work if they make us feel good, smart, and satisfied. Examples include feeling smart when we decide to eat healthy or buy something at a discount.

But we also engage internal incentives that relieve our pain or worry. Internal incentives do not have to be positive; they can simply be a decrease in a negative emotion. For example, if we are frustrated, we may take evasive action and quit trying; or if we are bored, we may distract ourselves with a video game. This self-soothing can habituate us to repeating that behavior. For example, while at Stanford doing research in Dr. Fogg's lab, a graduate student, Reeta Banerjee, and I did a study on the emotional side of why people use mobile apps. We found that people internally triggered their own app use 80 percent of the time, generally fueled by an internal tension like low-level anxiety (e.g., a sense of missing something or being bored). Think about all the internal, perhaps subconscious, triggers that cause you to impulsively check for e-mail, look up something that just popped into your head, or watch a different YouTube video—each of these satisfies a little itch of some kind—an anxiety, a curiosity, or a need to be busy.

A final type of internal incentive, aside from emotions of self-satisfaction or pain relief, involves competition. Some people find a great deal of satisfaction by competing with others, making it an internally rewarding experience. Competitions can also be mixed with external incentives, as in the case of trophies, awards, rankings, or prizes, making them very potent drivers for those who are inspired by competing.

TRUST, AND LOVE, WHO YOU ARE

The more you know yourself, the better designer you can be. The key here is to be realistic. I know that I have a slim chance of being a dainty, slow eater in this life—so anything I design has to work for that. I also know that my future self can be a very rebellious and crazy-busy "client." Therefore, I have to be careful not to overcommit her. Rather, I have to help her be in control (which my future self loves) and then leave room for her to be inspired to take it further if she is feeling up for it.

Maya Angelou once said, "Now that I know better, I do better." My meditation instructor, Sylvia, once explained in class how deep and drawn-out our ignorance or our not knowing better can be. Her view was consistent with Maya Angelou's.

"If we really truly knew better," she said, "we wouldn't do things that cause suffering. So if you are still doing that which causes suffering, you don't *really* know yet. You may have a notion that you know what you should do, but that is merely a surface concept—something to judge yourself or others. When we *really* know, when real wisdom is there, we simply stop."

This goes back to self-compassion. Not only do we show compassion to our future self by what we design for her, we have compassion when she breaks out of the design because she does not really know yet how to be better. No need to hate—rather, every reason to love her!

BUILDING ALIGNMENT

Approach building a healthy relationship, or alignment, with your future self as you would with anyone else—with shared respect, love, and attention. Make sure that your past self is a designer with compassion and empathy for the future self. I know I am repeating myself, but this cannot be overstated. And while the past self may provide compassionate and easy designs, these designs must also be airtight—because the future self will try to wriggle out of them. Your future self can and will rebel, relapse, or just plain be lazy. It can be distracted easily by all the other motivations and emotions it faces every second of every day.

When I was working with at-risk and incarcerated teens, a colleague of mine had a saying: "Don't tempt the innocent," which means, for example, do not leave your wallet out around people who are tempted to steal it. If you do, the breach is on you—you have played a part in bringing out that person's weakness by not being more careful. In the same way, you know your future self's weaknesses (because they are yours), and you can use this information to guard against temptations that bring them out. And, again, this is why we must iterate on and tweak our designs—so the future self likes the food and habitat that has been created for it, and it doesn't want to break out of the pen.

Rewards, self-appreciation, and celebration are other ways of aligning the past and future selves. They are natural steps in the design process. They are so natural that if you do not consciously build in reward, you may find yourself unconsciously celebrating in a way that undermines you. For example, whenever a friend of mine successfully eats healthfully for a while and drops a few pounds, she finds that she "rewards" herself by pigging out on birthday cake or whatever else is around during a party. What is that except celebrating success with cake and then undoing the success? Instead, if she consciously designed a healthy reward that would not sabotage her all the way back to the starting line, she may end this needless cycle of suffering.

To help reward your future self, go ahead and use incentives. Know that external incentives may be needed at first—to prime a new behavior perhaps. That's totally fine! Over time, if you can find personal meaning or pain relief by doing the new behavior, the incentive can become more internal, fueled from your own intrinsic motivation, and get solidified (myelinated) as a fast-brain habit. Be patient as this happens. Practice appreciation and gratitude to reward your past self so that you feel appreciated and encouraged to keep tweaking and iterating on the design. This builds self-trust, and just as Cynthia can ask her future self to execute a highly precise workout, you will pull your past and future selves into more alignment and harmony. No more messy self-sabotage, letting yourself down, breaking trust, hypocrisy, or other funks in the relationship—you are your own bestie!

Past self, future self

It's time for some good old relationship therapy between your past self and your future self. Let's have some fun while we learn and design for this, shall we? (And you'll remember it better that way too!)

Pretend your past self and future self are coming to you as their couples therapist. You will ask each of them to record their point of view, and then suggest what each of them could do to cooperate with each other better and be more harmonious with each other. Grab your journal and here we go!

PAST SELF'S POINT OF VIEW

Tell me, Past Self, what do you do (design) for Future Self that is meant to help but you feel doesn't get appreciated?

_____

_____

What do you wish Future Self would do differently in response to your hard work and effort on their behalf?

_____

_____

_____

_____

How do you think Future Self could improve how they are doing things?

_____

_____

_____

_____

FUTURE SELF'S POINT OF VIEW

Ok, Future Self, you heard that Past Self is trying to design things that are helpful for you. What is your experience of their designs? (Are their designs easy, difficult, complicated, expensive, unrealistic, or soothing to do?)

_____

_____

_____

What could Past Self do differently that would probably make you more willing to follow their designs for you?

_____

_____

_____

What are you willing to do going forward to
be more supportive of Past Self's efforts?

_____

_____

_____

THERAPIST'S POINT OF VIEW

Thank you both for sharing your experience
of one another. You are both clearly well
intentioned, good people who are trying their
best. In listening to you both, it sounds like a
good place for you to start getting closer and
becoming more collaborative would be: (finish
the sentence)

_____

_____

_____

Notes

⑨

got relapse? press reboot!

In nature, adaptation is important; the plan is not.

—*Laurence Gonzales*

"**O**h my god, I can't stand it! I feel like such a hypocrite!"

Susan was an insightful woman and a vocal member of a mothers of teenagers group that I trained in parent-teen communication a few years back. She was candid, and even self-critical, about her ongoing struggles with screaming at her teen daughter.

"Honestly, I don't know where the yelling comes from sometimes. It's just there. I hear it erupt and I can't stop it. It's like a part of me is watching the other part of me lay into her," her voice shook with sorrow, her eyes clamped onto tears.

Susan had shared stories with the group before about losing her patience with her daughter and the uncontrollable outbursts. On this particular evening, the tone had changed to one of desperation as she told us how she had promised her daughter that it would never ever happen again. She was inspired to make this change from our last session and had pledged aloud to everyone that she would change. But not even two days later, that promise had been broken. She had relapsed and felt out of control.

"I'm so ashamed about being a hypocrite like this. I wouldn't respect me if I were her either. I mean, would *you* respect me?"

Susan's tone was full of bitterness, directed at herself. Her face contorted as she said those last words, and we could all see that she was really suffering. I wanted to help her question where this harsh shame was coming from and, hopefully, to soften and release it. I felt strong compassion for her, having been in similar situations as a mother—how dreadful it feels to think that you are destroying your relationship with your child! But there was another, more toxic level to the suffering, one that was invisible to her but, in fact, is common to most people. Relapse into old behavior.

We are taught that relapse is a terrible thing, to be avoided at all costs, and is committed by only the weakest of people. How wrong!

"Susan," I began. "There's hope. Let's look at the pattern here. Since you started working on it, the yelling has gotten less frequent, right? I can tell that you are going longer and longer in between outbursts, right?"

She agreed.

I continued. "So I know, and I believe deep down you also know, that you're making progress."

Her head gave up some tiny, restrained nods, while the rest of the moms were nodding vigorously, trying to encourage her.

And that's just the thing. Susan's hesitation to celebrate her obvious-to-everyone-else improvement spoke volumes about the all-or-nothing thinking that we tend to apply to our own behavioral goals. We equate a misstep along the way to total failure. Susan had condemned her slippage into old yelling habits as a moral slaying by calling herself a hypocrite and feeling unworthy of respect. How tragic! And yet how common! The cultural adage "just do it" that we have learned unfortunately triggers many people to condemn themselves as weak, hypocritical, or not worthy of love when they relapse. Nothing could be farther from the truth, and I am here to convince you that relapse is as natural to change as exhaling is to breathing. So maybe for some people "just do it," would be more helpful if modified to "just do it again."

Relapse, or a re-emergence of the old default behavior, is a normal, natural, and sometimes necessary part of the behavior change process. I am not saying you should be cartwheels-level excited when it happens, but you can at least see it as a sign of progress. Remember our little baby wolf becoming the rival of the old established alpha wolf? This dynamic tension between the new behavior and the old default behavior is a positive sign of change. (Go, baby wolf, go!) But we know that the baby wolf's journey is not linear or without setbacks. The old alpha wolf of habits, like screaming at your daughter, rears its ugly head from time to time. When that happens, the baby wolf has to regain dominance, which it does because you help the baby wolf by iterating on your behavior design.

As ugly as it seems, relapse and hypocrisy can be positive indicators of change and progress. I know that sometimes people do not put themselves out there because they do not want to experience relapse or be judged as a hypocrite. For example, in private surveys, many more people care about preserving the environment for future generations than publicly stand up and claim it out loud. Why? They are afraid of not being 100 percent green—of someone pointing out when their new behaviors and old habits do not line up. Think back to what happened to Al Gore when he began boldly speaking out for the environment. Shortly thereafter, he was harshly criticized for leaving a large carbon footprint by flying to his speeches in a private jet. Ours can sometimes be a harsh world of judgment and all-or-nothing thinking. But that only comes from people who do not understand change.

Let's think back to what we learned about neuroplasticity in chapter 6, our chapter on sustaining change. As the new behavior is practiced more and more, the neural connections underlying that behavior get stronger and stronger. It is like wearing a rough footpath through repeated use, and then once established, paving that road (i.e., adding myelin to neural networks) to make it faster. Eventually there are two neural pathways that are of equal strength—the old habit and the new one—and you can imagine two highways that you could choose from. When we hit this point, the new behavior is as good an option (and equally likely to occur) as the old default behavior. Baby wolf is all grown up and challenging the alpha!

But here is where hypocrisy comes in. If the two wolves are of equal strength, if both highways are paved and equally fast options, we will use both! In this way, the hypocrisy of relapse is a legitimate phase of change in which we sometimes go the new way, the healthier way that we designed, but at other times we default down the old road we know so well. The tension between the two alternating behaviors is an outward sign of the competition between the two neural pathways. It is the struggle between our two wolves. Hypocrisy of behaviors is a good thing. All we have to do is keep focusing on and feeding the right wolf.

People watching from the outside can see us toggle back and forth between the two. I'm strong—I choose the healthy design. I'm tired or stressed—I default to unhealthy habits. So let's call hypocrisy the 50 percent mark, where both behaviors are equally likely to occur on any given day. We say one thing and we do another about half the time. That is how far Susan, our mother with the yelling habit, had made progress—only she couldn't see it for all her self-criticism.

Now let's think about the 100 percent mark. That's when the new behavior is well entrenched. It is 100 percent probable—or near to it. Basically, the new behavior takes over. It's embedded into our *Me* center of self-image; it's myelinated into the fast brain and burns no conscious mental energy. It's the fully-grown baby wolf who has challenged—and beaten—the old alpha.

But what do you think happens between the 50 percent mark and the almost always 100 percent mark? You guessed it. Lots of relapses!

THE POWER OF HOPE

Recognizing small successes along the way makes us more resilient and gives us hope. Let's consider an animal behavior study that makes this point so tangibly. Researchers who study how antidepressant drugs work commonly use an experimental task called the forced swim task. In this task, a mouse is placed in water and his movements are measured. If left for too long, the mouse gives up and, sadly, even drowns. But there is something that can keep him from drowning: hope. Studies show that if a human hand dips into the water to save the mouse or if he finds some means of escape by finding a ladder, then the time that the mouse is able to swim dramatically increases the next time he is tested.[51] Being saved gives the mouse hope, and with the power of hope, he can swim far longer. Mice that are given hope don't give up easily. They strive. Hope invigorates them. Animals (including us humans!) have neural machinery that turns on and helps us do amazing things when we have hope.

Maintaining hope requires building patience. They go hand-in-hand because we need them to both endure and stay effortful. But it can be hard to cultivate patience. I once met a monk at a friend's home who relayed this story about building patience:

> When I first became a monk, I was enthusiastic about sitting meditation. Every day, for hours at a time, I would devote myself to sitting on my cushion and quietly observing my mind. I thought that I was doing it 'right.'
>
> But then a year went on, then 2 and 3. Soon, 10 years later, I started to feel frustrated that, despite my devotion to my practice, I was not seeing progress in myself. So I went to my teacher, who had been meditating for over 60 years and asked him, 'Thay (teacher), I have

been sitting in meditation for years now, but I do not feel I am making enough progress. I still can't shake all of my bad habits.'

Thay kindly looked at me and gently asked, "Dear Brother, how long have you been sitting?"

For over 10 years now, I replied.

The teacher thoughtfully took in my answer and compassionately replied, "Oh, you've done really well. Give it another 20 years or so and you might see some changes."

I swallowed hard in disbelief, then silently laughed to myself at how impatient I had been to get rid of my old behaviors instead of just experiencing the process of my transformation.

What the monk's teacher had said was at first shocking (20 years!), yet his dismay was quickly replaced by relief—and hope. In a brief moment, his teacher had dismantled his rush to improve by stretching the timeline beyond his fixed expectations. His teacher's words invited his mind to let go of the "project" of successful meditation.

This is the mind of the designer—patiently experiment and experience, continuously iterate and redesign.

Tinker and tweak. Extend the deadline. Even Franklin D. Roosevelt said, "It is common sense to take a method and try it: If it fails, admit it frankly and try another. But above all, try something." We also see this mindset in colloquialisms like one of my grandmother's favorites, "God isn't finished with me yet."

When we design for behavior change, it can be so easy to get fixated on the outcome. It's not that it's bad to have an expectation of where we're going—not at all. We are not just floating out in space with no direction or aim. We absolutely should have a point of view and set an intention so that we are resolute and don't spin in indecision.

But when the rigid, fixed goal starts to be used as a weapon against ourselves, it is time to think like a designer and reframe it. Approach the goal as a version 1.0 prototype that is expected to improve in future iterations. This helps us hold it with a firm but sensitive grip. It is like the colloquialism, "If you hold a bird in your hand too tightly, you will kill it, but if you hold it too loosely, it will fly away."

Designing your behavior sits at the tender balance point between clear goals and openness—it's about bringing your full effort alongside full flexibility.

RELAPSE

In our society, *relapse* is a dirty word. It is typically assigned to people who are broken, addicted, or weak in willpower. Admittedly, some kinds of relapses can be harmful, even deadly, so it makes sense that they would be perceived so negatively. But it is time to change this perception, because nothing could be more natural and necessary as we course through the sometimes bumpy stages of change. As we understood with neuroplasticity and the metaphor of the two wolves in chapter 6, the old alpha wolf sometimes comes roaring back—this is a given. Neuroplasticity does not cause immediate or easy dismantling of this old alpha as the default neural network for quite some time. No wonder we relapse—it's just sitting there ready to happen!

From a neuroplasticity point of view, a relapse is simply a set of competing neural pathways in your brain that causes two (or more) alternate behaviors to toggle back and forth. And it turns out that the biggest determinant of what you will do is context. This was only recently discovered using behaviors from a most unusual example: the nematode worm.

Nematode worms are one of scientists' favorite animals to study because they are simple, easy to breed, and well documented. In particular, they provide a useful model of understanding neuroscience because they have only about 300 neurons, in comparison to the human brain, which has over 100 billion! This means that scientists can figure out when each of the nematode's neurons are active and which ones are wired to which other ones (aka a complete connectome of wiring).

Dr. Andrew Leifer's lab at Princeton University has discovered the biggest thing that predicts the nematode's next behavior: what just happened to it. In its simple life, the nematode has only a few behaviors to choose from. When something happens to the nematode, it sets off the next behavior, which then sets off the next behavior—like a chain reaction. It is fairly predictable.

But, really, how much more advanced are we? As we covered in chapter 3, human behavior is susceptible to priming, a heuristic in the fast brain that strongly influences what we do next. We can be primed to be insecure, worried, prejudiced, generous, and many other expressed feelings and behaviors. And we react predictably—just like a nematode.

With this in mind, let's revisit relapse. The old behavior, the relapse, is always set off by some sort of context, whether triggering, priming, or other heuristic (brain shortcut).

Here are some common contexts that can cause relapse:

- You get distracted: You're working on that project on your computer and—oops—you ate the whole bowl, bag, or box of that snack you cannot resist. How did that happen? Any little thing that fractures your attention opens the door to relapse. Other attention-shattering contexts include lack of sleep, stress, multi-tasking, and not being sober.

- You are ruminating: Relapse does not come out of the clear blue sky. Instead, you were probably ruminating, with your thoughts playing in a loop in your brain (consciously or unconsciously) long before you acted on them. You know how it goes, *Look at those cupcakes! Oh, that looks so good. But no, I shouldn't—oh, but I really want to! How about I buy one and only eat half?* Then you order two cupcakes. Such ruminating builds tension and can quickly detonate into action, with you (your slow brain) coming to your senses only as you lick the last crumb off the wrapper.

- You get triggered: Strong emotions can and will trigger you to relapse. For example, you go through a nasty breakup and immediately relapse into your old party habits. Your environment also provides another source of triggers to relapse. Just think of how you have acted when you were back at your childhood home around family. Did any one of your parents or siblings trigger you to relapse into old patterns or less flattering behaviors? Enough said. A strong trigger field like that can throw even the most developed and highly successful people into remedial relapse.

ACCEPTING RELAPSE

Now that you know the likelihood of relapse is 100 percent, you can easily see that you have to design for it. The first admission to make as a designer is that you are somewhat addicted to your old alpha wolf behavior. Despite the harm that your old behavior is causing in the present, it is there because in the past it somehow helped you cope or survive. It made you feel normal and became part of your *Me*. We are all addicts to the feeling of familiar, comfortable *Me*, no matter how dysfunctional *Me* was.

The second admission to make is that you will relapse. I am not talking about saying you know you will relapse, but truly accepting it as much as possible before it happens. This is super important. Why? Because I want to minimize the time you spend off the wagon before you get back on it! People can wallow in relapse and denial of relapse for years! Admit it—get back on the wagon—simple.

I once knew a woman, Allison (not her real name), who was a social butterfly and knew everyone in town. Everyone loved her. She organized things for her local community, volunteered at the school, and gathered parents for self-help workshops. But her dad was dying way across the continent and Allison started to act differently. Her friends noticed she was flaking on commitments. She was caught in a white lie or two.

Then on one late night, she called me crying from the Denver airport. She had flown with her daughter to see her ill father and on their way back their connecting flight was canceled and she was stuck, penniless, in the airport until the next day. I felt incredible compassion. I did not have much money in those days, but I called a hotel, gave them my credit card, and told them she could order room service to eat. I hung up and felt relieved.

But once I saw my credit card bill, I was furious! Allison had charged hundreds of dollars of food, liquor, and in-room movies in just under twelve hours. Stunned that anyone would do this to someone who helped them, I called and confronted her.

At the time, I did not know that I was dealing with a relapse—in this case, a relapse into prescription drugs and alcohol. People who have lived with addicts would have recognized this behavior in a hot second, but it was my first time. Allison's relapse had slowly evolved over the previous weeks, getting stronger and stronger with each lie that she told her friends and colleagues. Her strong desire not to be relapsing prevented her from admitting and designing for the relapse, and caused her to alienate those who wanted to support her. Instead, she experienced, and caused, tremendous suffering by running from the truth and equating her relapse to a failure rather than a signal to get help.

The bottom line is plan for relapses. If you do not,

the hurt will come like it did for Allison. Don't ever make life chase and pin you down until you cry *Uncle* to shake you out of your denial—because it will!

What I've just described is what I believe is the weakness of many popular behavior change models. For example, James Prochaska's transtheoretical model of behavior change[52] is a psychotherapy-inspired model that assesses people's willingness and commitment to change their behaviors. The stages are precontemplation (not ready for change), contemplation (getting ready), preparation (ready), action, maintenance, and termination. The maintenance stage is, if we were talking about a fairy tale, the "they lived happily ever after" part and the scene would draw to a tidy close. But there is no mention of relapse and its inevitability. No plan is offered on how to recover from relapse. The behavior change story painted by Prochaska proceeds along a linear progression and ends with success—forever.

But that's not real life. That's not neuroplasticity either.

In real life, relapse happens more often than not. This is not admitting defeat right out of the gate; it is about being proactive! The biggest oversight in the current models of behavior change is not designing a plan for how to recover from a relapse.

It's time to quit pretending that once we are ready, we carry out our plan to perfection, reach our goal, and, cruising long, we just maintain it steadily from there. That basically never happens. Very few people go cold turkey, overnight, forever. And if they do stop cold turkey for one behavior, like smoking, they cannot reliably do it for everything else they want to change. Change, as a process, is a very bumpy path. It is like a bunny hop—three hops forward, two hops back. Always remember that real progress goes up and down, reflective of the gradual brain changes that are working beneath the surface to establish your new neural network (new alpha wolf) over time.

Here's what I want for you: if you expect to relapse, you will stop judging or shaming yourself when it does (inevitably) happen. You'll be more accepting and more relaxed and therefore better able to activate and respond appropriately to the situation, rather than defend yourself or try to escape. You will not spin in shame or confusion anymore; rather you will know exactly what is happening and be clear that you need to feed that baby wolf right away! Finally, you will feel free from failure, steer clear of the habenula's condemnation, and iterate your way out of any personal form of hell you find yourself in. May it be so!

DESIGN YOUR WAY OUT OF A RELAPSE

I often fantasize about developing an antishame spray to simply and quickly dissolve that sludge of shame, much like cleansers in commercials that are sprayed on shower mildew, which just drips off to reveal the shiny beauty underneath. I want an antishame spray because I have noticed that shame, even more than past failures, is the number one reason people stop designing and iterating on their life. They are embarrassed that they used to be doing so well but "now look at me." Remember the after-school tutor from chapter 1 who was biking to work, doing yoga, and eating healthy only to end up a year later completely baffled by how she relapsed. But what's worse, she was visibly ashamed that she was back to square one.

Let's play with the imaginary formulation of such an antishame spray. What would the key ingredient of the spray be? Iteration! "I'm iterating, not failing." Another active ingredient would be reframing—if we can reframe our suffering into some greater context or purpose, then we don't have to shame our self. "What is this teaching me?" Finally, the spray would contain validation—to replenish a balanced view of who you really are with all the positive qualities and intentions you have. "I am a good person doing the best I can." And here is how I would want the warning about its side effects to read: "Warning! May cause clarity. The design has failed, not you!"

My point is that the key to designing ourselves out of a relapse is to neutralize shame and reignite the willingness to iterate. So, sans an actual spray, here is what I learned about what works for addressing shame and recovering from relapse—taught to me by gang member youths.

Let's go back to what I mentioned in the last chapter about incarcerated youths who had every sincere intention to change their negative behaviors while in juvenile hall. Over and over again, I experienced these young men to be so heartbroken, contrite, and earnest. I believed 100 percent that they wanted to get out of their gang and escape street life—not out of naiveté—out of the truth that existed in them at that moment and in that context. We would talk about it for months prior to their release, and I thought I was doing all that I could to help prepare and fortify them. Fast forward. They would get out and immediately the street would engulf them again. The environmental trigger field was just too much for their good intentions, and the old alpha wolf came roaring back with a vengeance.

Before they got out, I would make an appointment with each young man to meet me after his court release so we could spend the day getting him enrolled in school again. I even took the time to attend their court release dates. But only a few hours later, when I went to their house to pick them up for our appointment, they had flipped back into street mode. They didn't pick up the phone when I called. Some even pretended not to be at home while I stood there knocking on the door awkwardly, sticking out like a sore thumb in the housing projects, while onlooker gang members stared at me. I was confused by this hypocrisy—in the deepest part of their heart, I *knew* that each of them wanted to change. I believed in them. Why did they avoid me?

It took me years to figure out what had happened to them. These youth had relapsed, and they were immediately crippled with shame. I was a witness to their most private hopes and inner goodness in a moment of vulnerability—and then watched them metamorphose into the worst side of themselves. They could not face me. I was the living reminder of all their good intentions gone sour. During their relapse, overwhelmed with feelings of worthlessness, they ran farther away from anything and anyone helpful. Locked in a big fat shame bubble, they were unreachable.

Now, it's easy to judge these youths for not doing what they said they would do. But how is that any different from any of the other stories in this book of people who know what they should do but don't do it? Everyone does this at one time or another—it's the same pattern. The difference is that a relapsing gang member or addict may cause serious harm to themselves or others whereas someone else's relapse into a different problem behavior like overeating may result in gaining a few pounds.

Regardless, whether young or old, male or female, we all fall into the fast brain–slow brain gap at some point. That gap applies to all of us, yet it doesn't make any of us less sincere about wanting to change deep down inside. Know the difference between good intentions and bad actions—and don't discount or discredit the good intentions of yourself or others just because the fast brain–slow brain gap is gobbling them up at the moment.

But here was what the youths' relapse patterns taught me about recovering and trying again. As I mentioned, relapse in this population meant incarceration or sometimes violent death, so the stakes were very, very high.

Because of the extreme nature of their relapses, I was able to see with high fidelity what was true about relapse for all of them—and later realized was true for all people in relapse. I came up with a recipe—a design recipe if you will—for how to unstick anyone who is relapsing. It worked. In my final full-time year of working with them, I counted up the recidivism rates in the youths our organization helped after release versus those who received help from the standard probation services—we had a far lower recidivism rate of 25 percent compared to the control group with 87 percent return to incarceration.

So, what's the recipe? Basically, someone who is relapsing needs to understand three things to have the hope and confidence to resume their efforts:

1. You're not bad.
2. You're not alone.
3. There's a way out.

If we can check off the boxes for these three relapse needs, we can abate or sidestep the shame just enough to iterate toward another solution. Let's go through each.

YOU'RE NOT BAD

Everyone needs to know that there is hope for them, that they are a good person. I have worked with some of the most violent, angry people in our society who have done some of the worst things imaginable. But even they deserve and need to feel like they are not fundamentally bad in order to turn a new leaf and work to build the positive side of themselves and their behaviors. I get it that some people would rather have people who have done horrible things know how horrible they are for the rest of their lives. I have tremendous compassion for people who want others to be punished so harshly, knowing that they themselves are in tremendous pain or else they wouldn't want to be so vindicated. What they may not know is that the person they want to suffer is already suffering—having suffered incredible abuse or neglect as a child—or else they wouldn't be like they are (the exception being those who have psychoses and other mental disabilities). And it doesn't mean that they are getting away with anything.

I once saw a drawing from an incarcerated youth that showed a picture of a teenage boy huddled in the corner of his cell crying at night. The caption said, "If people knew the suffering inside of me, they would not wish for any more punishment, realizing it's enough." Regardless of what you believe about punishment or forgiveness and who it helps or hurts, the bottom line is this—we all need compassion, for ourselves and ideally from others, to do better.

It is a paradox, really. For years we have been taught "no pain, no gain." And this is a very good slogan if (a) the pain is short, and (b) we are on our way to something inspiring or self-satisfying. But when it comes to self-flogging (or blaming others) because we (or they) did not do what we (or they) should, inflicting more pain just causes us (or them) to shut down. When people—even the worst people—experience more pain when they are already suffering, it just hardens them further. The only way to get ourselves or others to change is through grace in the form of compassion, hope, or relief. Fundamentally, we have to believe that we are not bad so that we can muster the courage to get back up from our relapse and practice being our better selves.

In my work designing health and wellness programs for people, I deal with this all the time. Many times my firm is hired by an organization that needs to change behaviors for a specific group of people—let's say people with type 2 diabetes. They hire us because they have not been successful at getting this population of people to take better care of their disease. And what we often find is that they have been communicating to the collective shame of their intended audience—not intentionally, accidentally! For example, they may have sent e-mails that lead with a message like "We can help you manage your diabetes and weight." Excuse me? Have we met?

This type of message is problematic for a number of reasons. First, no one wants to receive help—we all want to be the one giving help. "So, are you telling me I need help, that I am 'bad?' No thank you!" Second, no one wants to be known for their greatest weakness—in this case, being overweight and having a disease that makes them vulnerable. "Thanks for pointing that out—I will now avoid you because you are brutishly stomping on my shame." Finally, who is *we* and *you*? By calling me *you*, I am already being patronized and not a part of a group—we are not in this together. It's me and you—dichotomous, distant, other.

This is how we talk. To others. To ourselves privately in our heads. It can be subtle but so exacting and impactful. We need to undo this with the simple medicine of "not bad."

Here's why you aren't bad (or lazy, or worthless, or hypocritical, or any other variety of self-hatred and judgment). With the fast brain–slow brain gap, there is a lag between when we relapse and when we realize that we have relapsed. This gap means that sometimes the cookie is in your mouth before you remember that you promised not to eat cookies. Remember that you are on your way to reducing the gap. You are always making the gap smaller by courageously and continuously practicing awareness. You can catch a relapse after it has happened with less and less of a time lapse until, eventually, you are aware of it just before it is about to happen, which is the all-powerful moment that you can prevent the relapse. How empowering!

Here's another reason you are not bad—you can and do change all the time. Although you cannot point to dramatic or external changes and therefore you may think you never change, the truth is that you are always changing. You're literally not the same person. You are a dynamic, ever-changing being. Almost all the molecules in your body have been completely replaced just during the past three months! There's nothing left of what you call yourself from even a few years ago—everything is new, turned over and updated. The constant redesign of your tissues and your very molecular structure is a metaphor for how change is ongoing and inevitable, with or without you designing for it. It's your choice: let it happen or make it happen.

Knowing this, I forbid you to say that you'll never change. Every day is a new start. Now, I don't mean that in some woo-woo, mystical sense. We're talking science here! You are a vibrant, ever-changing, dynamic being, who is capable of incredible changes—so give yourself permission to drop the idea that you are somehow wrong or bad or a failure when you relapse.

We have the opportunity to reboot our lives in any way and at any time that we choose. All the behaviors we do are by choice. Doing nothing is a choice too. If we choose to do nothing, we still change—just not by intention, not by design—and we probably won't like the direction the change takes us. We just drift. We gain a few pounds a year. Maybe we get progressively more miserable in our job or relationship. Our muscles and strength waste away. Those are all changes too. But why wouldn't you rather steer that natural, inevitable stream of change toward what you want instead of letting it morph into something you don't want?

Let's recall that concept in Buddhist philosophy known as beginner's mind. This idea encourages us to approach each experience as a beginner, bringing all the curiosity and open-mindedness and nonjudgment of a total novice. Expectations that we have to be this perfect all-knowing expert are simply arrogant. Beginner's mind helps reboot people when they relapse because it sets the expectation that they are still learning like an enthusiastic child would. It eases the pressure of "should have known better" and gives us another really good reason to believe we are not bad.

YOU'RE NOT ALONE

There are some amazingly inspirational stories of overcoming failure out there. Did you know that Walt Disney was fired from his newspaper job because his boss said he lacked imagination, and that early in her career, Oprah was advised to get out of the business because she was completely unfit for journalism? Did you know that *Harry Potter* novelist and billionaire J. K. Rowling once got canned for being a daydreamer, and that the inventor of the Dyson vacuum cleaner found what worked best after a mere 5,127 failed prototypes of the machine?

Really successful people fail and relapse all the time. We just forget this. Or maybe we have a nasty habit of idealizing others because it gives us some excuse to stay small. "I couldn't possibly be as good as they are." Either way, we mistakenly get the impression that we are alone in our relapsing.

One way we isolate ourselves is by thinking others do not have the same issues. If you think someone else does not struggle with relapse, there is one of two things going on. Either you just don't know them well enough to watch them go through it, or they are hiding it out of their own shame. Either way, if others' relapses are hidden from us, we may idealize those people by putting them on a pedestal or use their seeming perfection as an excuse to indulge self-loathing and isolation.

As humans, we absolutely need others. We are built to be social. Our brains reflect that. We are equipped with mirror neurons, which are neurons that take everything we see another person do and play it out in our own brain as if we were doing it.

Mirror neurons were discovered during experiments with primates, where one macaque's brain was hooked up to a recording device while the scientists were setting up the experiment.[53] He happened to be watching the other macaque in the experiment eat a banana and the exact region of his brain (rostral inferior premotor cortex) was active as if he himself were eating the banana! In other words, the activity recorded in the brain of the monkey who was merely observing the other monkey's behavior mirrored the brain activity of that active monkey.

OK, so here's my off-the-record, unproven hypothesis about why people watch Sunday NFL games. I think that viewers, particularly men, enjoy watching professional athletes make amazing maneuvers because of the catharsis and pleasure they feel from their own mirror neurons activating as if they were personally performing those amazing athletic feats.

For women, the equivalent may be vicariously watching emotionally dramatic or romantic shows, like *The Bachelor*, because the female brain is far more activated by gossip and social tension.[54] I am ashamed to admit that I occasionally get sucked in—not the best use of my mirror neurons, yah?

We are wired to be social. Even introverts—they just need some downtime to recover. I do not mean that we have to be broadcasting everything on social media to be social. In fact, a very large study on happiness by UC Berkeley Greater Good Science Center researchers Emiliana Simon-Thomas and Matt Killingsworth reveal interesting findings on what makes us happy with respect to social experiences. In their study of over 65,000 volunteer participants worldwide, they found that we are happiest (a) when we are with other people, (b) when we are interacting with those people, and (c) when we are with friends and loved ones.[55] In health outcomes research, this is further supported by the disparity of better outcomes for those who have social support systems versus those who do not, even given the same type and amount of disease.

So now that we are convinced that we are interdependent with other humans and that everyone relapses, let's put it together. The cure for the isolation and shame that happens with relapse is the power of groups. The power of being in a group of like-minded people who are nonjudgmental and supportive protects against relapse. People get back up faster when there is someone right there who has been there. "I've been there too" is a quick recovery salve for the sting of relapse. Without this, we can wallow in our self-pity, worthlessness, or shame forever!

You are not alone. Learn from others who have been there. There is nothing you could ever experience that another human being hasn't done, felt, or experienced. Find your tribe. Lean on them when you fall—and get back on your path!

THERE'S A WAY OUT

When we relapse, sometimes it feels like all is lost. All the doors are closed—slammed shut! Like being in a power outage, it's important to acknowledge that you are indeed in darkness. People tend to think of darkness as a bad place because there is a groundlessness and uncertainty to it—a sense of not knowing what's coming next. This fear can lead some people to lose hope and get stuck in the dark. When it feels this bleak, it's time to seek—for the lesson, for the light, for the way out.

In 1999, I lost hope. I had always been an incredibly stable and strong person, the one everyone else relied on, even helping to rescue fellow students in medical school who had fallen into depression and suicidal ideation. I had a lot of compassion for them but couldn't relate to feeling so low that you wanted to die. I never dreamed I would ever be susceptible to such thoughts.

But then I met my darkness.

My closest friend and cofounder of our nonprofit and I had a falling out. It doesn't matter now who did what—responsibilities for bad relationships are always inter-twined. Suffice it to say we were the closest of friends who depended on each other for everything and spoke every day, and then suddenly we didn't speak at all. I felt that all doors had closed, my identity was gone, and there was no way for me to move forward without her.

I fell into depression. I remember telling my husband at the time that I felt unrelentingly sad. Strangely, I could not feel joy. That was new. I had two super cute little daughters who did fun and cute things several times a day, but I was like a numb zombie who could not enjoy or feel their happiness.

I started to worry about myself for the first time in my life. I was starting to think about death—a lot. I did not have a plan to commit suicide; it was more like I wanted to passively die or be killed. My husband was worried too. I was unnerved most by seeing his concern for me. No one had ever been worried about me before. I told him that I needed to take time to myself in nature—and he agreed because he wanted me to get better. And so did I.

Truly, this was a relapse into depressive thinking that far surpassed my prior experiences. I certainly was depressive episodically in high school, mostly situational due to stress of my parents' divorce, family conflict, my compulsive eating, and self-loathing. So, I had tasted depression, but I had not ever felt this hopeless and certainly had never entertained the idea of wanting my life to end. I was terrified by this more extreme level of depression, which felt out-of-control and unfixable to me—like I had no way out.

I have always felt very close to my Native American ancestry, so I tend to address my psychological needs with healing time in nature. Dealing with this very new experience of suicidal thoughts, my instinct was to start spending one night per week outside in the state park near my house. My husband reluctantly supported me. Every Wednesday, I would take a sleeping bag with me into the park at dusk and spend the night because, after all, I still had to go to work in the morning and take care of my kids in the evening. This went on for about three months. But it wasn't resolving how I felt. I decided to take things up a notch.

This one particular Wednesday, there was a wind-storm. I decided to climb up the mountain this time—hoping that the elevation would help me pick my mind up off the ground. So at dusk I strapped my sleeping bag to my back, walked into the thousand-acre park, and started to climb the foothills of Mount Diablo (the symbology of Devil Mountain was not lost on me). The wind was blowing uncharacteristically hard for our area. I thought to myself that the noise of the wind would be a disadvantage for me to detect predators like coyotes, or, worse, mountain lions. As I was thinking this, I came around a bend in the trail to find two men hiking down the hill. They were a bit sketchy—not the REI poster boys that I would have trusted, but rougher—were they hunters? Would they hunt me? When out in nature, I have always been more afraid of men than mountain lions.

Forcing myself not to look back at them, I trudged upward. The foliage changed from grass and brush to large pine trees and manzanitas. I was amazed by the beautiful silhouettes of the giant pines around me, simultaneously in awe and in fear. And they were to be feared—these were 70-foot-tall Coulter pines, covered in 16-inch, 10-pound pinecones with sharp spikes. In the wind, the pinecones were dropping around me like head-splitting bombs from the dark sky. There was no way to protect myself should one fall. I was convinced the sharp spikes could rip the skin down my face if they fell just so.

Tired of hiking, I finally sat under one of the tallest pines. Crazy, right? Well, yes! In my numbness, I didn't care. I wanted to die—to have one of the pinecones take me out. At the same time, I could feel pure fear—a faint sign that I was not deadened. Then things got worse.

At first, I heard some twigs snap in the brush behind me. A chill went up the back of my neck. I was being watched. From the patterns of the sounds, movement and stillness, I knew it was a cougar. I thought, *Do it! Do it!* But the lion just sat there, crouched in the darkness, while my mind toggled between death-by-pinecone and death-by-cougar.

Time froze. I froze. For hours, I sat paralyzed with fear through the black night—my only movement being the shaking of my body from the cold since I did not bother pulling out my sleeping bag with a cougar 20 feet away. What would be the point? The Coulters continued to pitch and sway above me in the wind, occasionally launching one of their deadly pine cones to stab the ground around me like a knife thrower in a carnival act.

My fear grew with every minute. The cougar stayed put. The wind continued to blow. The Coulters continued to drop their bombs. I was terrified, but at the same time I was grateful to feel again. Finally, I felt something stronger than sadness for the first time in what seemed like forever! As this feeling intensified, I became aware of a deeper source underlying the fear—I wanted to live!

Then the rustling started again in the brush behind me. I was done with this. Still shaking from fear and cold and lack of sleep, I stood up and turned to face my predator. "Go away!" I screamed over and over, making myself as big as I could. The rustling paused, then moved, then paused, then moved. The cougar was slinking off.

A few hours later, a dim glow started behind the eastern foothills. It grew and grew. My heart filled with hope and gratitude for my survival, not just literally but metaphorically—I wanted to be here again. I wanted to see my babies again and hug and kiss and play with them! The final peak of light crested over the top of the ridge, casting a beam of sunlight so brilliant that it seemed pointed only at me—warming my face, my smiling, tear-dripping face. I crawled over to the brush where the cougar had been, confirmed the size and shape of the tracks, and gave thanks for his medicine. Then I walked down the mountain and back into life.

During a relapse and in our darkest hours, we all need to know that there is a way out. It is an essential ingredient for us to resume our efforts to change and design our behavior. A way out can be many things. In my story, it was the intensity of my fear giving way to the hope of sunlight. For others, it could be advice from a friend, an opportunity from an unexpected source, or a generous gift. Still for others, it could be going on retreat or taking antidepressants. I am not a purist. The way out that gives people the hope and courage to get back into action is specific to each individual. I am a strong advocate for open-mindedness because the answer could come from anyone and anywhere and be in any form. It reminds me of the parable of two frogs.

An old parable tells of two frogs that fell into a jug of milk. The first frog loses hope. He gives up and dies. The second frog keeps kicking and never gives up. He frantically moves his body as he searches for the way out. All of this movement starts to churn the milk, eventually turning it into butter. When it is solid enough, he gets his footing and jumps out to safety.

Nothing stays the same forever, and there is always a way out. The way out may be immediate or it may take a long time. It may be apparent or it may be a mystery. You may have to stay in motion or you may have to be still. You may have to use faith or you may have to lose faith. But approaching each situation with the mindset of a designer, expecting to relapse and expecting to iterate on your design, will protect you and help you, and you'll figure out how to churn your way out of any crisis.

Don't ever, ever give up!

Recovering from a relapse is all about effort. In a way, it is binary—you're either trying or you're not. The trick is to get ourselves not to give up, to just keep persevering no matter what.

When I think of true perseverance, I always remember David Lewis, a mentor and dear friend to me, an inspiration who is the ultimate story of rising up like a phoenix. David was a social entrepreneur and international executive trainer. He completely remade himself after being sentenced as a 16-year-old to San Quentin Prison for drug possession, where he served 15 years. He got clean from drugs while in prison by becoming a peace-loving, self-disciplined Muslim. (Crimes by radical Islamists have nothing to do with the majority of loving, devoted, chaste, and peaceful Muslims.) Once he got out, he relapsed because there were no services or jobs for someone like him. Featured in the "Circle of Recovery" documentary by Bill Moyers, David beat the odds and regained his sobriety, along with trade union employment. Based on what he learned, he started a 12-step substance recovery center called Free At Last in East Palo Alto, which, at the time, had the distinction of being the murder capital of the United States. Not only did David successfully build the center, raise funds, and save lives at Free At Last, he leveraged his intellect, charisma, and likeability to become an international corporate leadership trainer and speaker. Standing 6 foot 5 with a muscular build and dark skin, David added to his Atlas-like personal brand with a shaved head and salt-and-pepper handlebar mustache. To a stranger, David might have been intimidating. To those who knew him, however, he was a teacher and humble servant of humanity.

I have never known anyone with more grit, grace, and get-real profundity than David. He and I met at the Echoing Green All Fellows Conference when I was running a nonprofit—or perhaps I should say that the nonprofit was running me. He was 14 years my senior and had formed his nonprofit five years prior. I was just starting out as a social entrepreneur and the workload, emotional load, and financial struggle was more intense than anything I had ever done before (including med-ical school!). I was feeling burned out—fried, actually. We talked for a while, about the work, about the youth, about the scarcity of funding.

Maybe because I was desperate and unable to hide it anymore, I finally asked David what was really on my mind.

"What do you do when you think that, maybe, you're going to burn out?" I felt shame to hear myself say the words.

I expected him to either chastise me for not being a good social entrepreneur or tell me to suck it up. Even worse, I cringed at the thought that he would be disgusted by my weakness and tell me to quit. He did none of this.

David sternly examined my face for what felt like forever. I wasn't sure what he was looking for, but I knew he had figured out how to read people very well while in prison—where life and death are often determined by that skill.

Then he cracked a smirk.

"Ah, HELL. I done burned out YEARS ago! I burned out so bad there whatn' nothin' left of me!" He paused for a moment before continuing. "If you burn out—you just work from the ashes, darlin'! Just gotta work it from them ashes!" He chuckled as he spoke the last part.

What a testimony to iteration and the mindset of a designer—David was a brilliant behavior designer, although he did not call it that.

And he walked the walk! David, despite his international travel and fame, always made it a point to personally pick up new clients to his program on the day of their release from prison. "It keeps me grounded," he used to say.

Tragically, David's triumphant life and service to others was cut short when a schizophrenic friend having paranoid hallucinations fatally shot him outside of his car at an upscale mall parking lot. The world lost a powerful soul whose message was to work from the ashes, to continue on no matter how dark it gets. This was evidenced when over a thousand people attended his funeral to give thanks for the impact David had on their life—something that lives on beautifully in each of us.

Shortly after his death, I was missing David so I thought I would call his voicemail just to hear his outgoing message of wisdom (paraphrased from my memory): "Hey, leave me a message and I'll get back to you—and—don't NEVER give up—NO MATTER WHAT!"

I haven't. And neither can you.

Rebooting

Here is a way to reboot yourself into designing and reiterating after a relapse. For each of the reboot needs, you will self-diagnose and then write out a message to yourself that you will open sometime in the future.

NOTE TO SELF: YOU ARE NOT BAD.

Write a letter, note, or e-mail to your future self as if you were a compassionate friend. Describe all the ways in which your future self is not bad for relapsing. Perhaps emphasize the importance of the effort you have already made and remind yourself that relapse is part of the neuroplasticity process. Recall all the ways in which you are a positive, loving, giving, and effortful person. Encourage yourself so that you know you can and will figure this out. Try to reframe any areas where you judge yourself harshly, again assuming the gentle tone of a compassionate friend.

Put this message in a time capsule. You can set an e-mail that will be sent in the future (see end of section on how), have a friend or spouse give or mail you the message when they see you relapse, or just put it someplace where you can reach for it when the time is ripe.

NOTE TO SELF: YOU ARE NOT ALONE.

Again, write something to your relapsed future self. In this message, think of all the reasons you are not alone. List the people who care about you, the supports that exist, and suggestions on how to find people who have been through similar relapses. Give a few ideas of where to go, whom to call, or what to read or watch that would help you feel not so alone. Include any contact information that makes it easier for your future self to take action and encourage your future self to reach out in ways that address any reluctance or resistance to do so.

Again, put this message in a time capsule in a way that will get your future self's attention.

NOTE TO SELF: THERE IS A WAY OUT!

What can you say to your relapsing future self that would cut through fear, shame, doubt, or disappointment? What would get your future self to feel hope and see a way out of the darkness? What resources, therapists, support groups, or other methods would be healing and restorative so your future self will not give up? Write this down in a way that will ease the heart and get the attention of your future self as you did in the first two exercises above.

As part of the design for these exercises, set a trigger that will get your future self's attention. Asking another person to give you the message when you relapse often works. You can also self-serve these triggers. At the time of this writing, there are e-mail services like www.futureme.org and www.whensend.com where you can write an e-mail to yourself for delivery in the future. You can also send snail mail with the help of a friend, or you can just stack up a bunch of these in sealed envelopes with a title like "Open Me When You

Feel Alone" and put them in a basket on your dresser (like I did).

You can do this! And remember, don't give up—no matter what! *smile

Notes

⑩

freeing from attachment

When I let go of what I am,
I become what I might be.

—Lao Tzu

Like many of us, one of my dearest friends enjoys a good glass of wine. Over the last couple of years, her enjoyment had gone from drinking a glass at dinner parties to continuing to sip wine throughout the evening until bedtime. This increase had been quite gradual, and she did not seem to be impaired by it—no financial or relationship impact as far as she could tell—but the growing consistency of it was causing her concern. She brought it up to me one day when she said she had to call the drinking a habit, one that was growing into a bigger and stronger alpha wolf.

"I used to drink wine to take the edge off, but it's every night now," she said.

"Could you stop drinking if you wanted to?" I said, shifting into my clinical mindset a little.

"Yeah, I think so. But that's the thing. I rarely take a night off from it... so I guess that means I don't really want to stop," she thoughtfully replied.

Like the tip of the iceberg, I could tell these words only tapped into a little bit of her distress around her drinking pattern. She was worried that it was becoming an addiction.

"I don't know where this came from," she continued. Also like the tip of such a massive block of ice, there was a lot submerged here that wasn't conscious at the surface. And that's the case with many behavior patterns. So we dove in to see what was underneath the surface.

"Let's start with *why*," I led in. "What need does the wine fulfill? Loneliness? Stress? What does it symbolize to you?"

She paused to consider.

"I guess it helps me to blow off steam. My life is so busy and regimented, it gives me the one time when I don't have to be anywhere or do anything for anyone," she exhaled, revealing some of the "steam" she still had built up inside of her. This made sense because I knew she was working full-time, going to school full-time, and had been going nonstop without a social life for the past two years. No wonder she wanted a break from being so overly responsible! Her future self was saying, "hell no!" to all the discipline and constant work. Some part of her wanted to play, but she was too busy to take the time to go out with friends or even go on dates—the wine had become her private vacation from it all.

And it goes deeper than that because the drinking, in a way, wasn't the real issue at all. The true issue lay beneath the surface. Consuming the wine expressed merely a symptom of something more insidious—the needs that are fulfilled by the behavior.

We started to examine what needs the wine drinking met. In addition to her stated need to "blow off steam," which indicated high pressure and stress within, we identified that she also wanted to rebel a little against how disciplined she had been. Her "inner teen" was rejecting the control of her strong frontal lobe that was running her life. Finally, there was a *Me* component. Her dad had passed away a few years ago and, being an alcoholic himself, had roped her in to drinking after work when she visited him daily. She had gone along with it because it was the only way to bond with her dad—so her brain was making the association between the wine and her connection with her dad.

You can see the tangled web that wove its way around her. The psychological and emotional needs had "designed" this behavior in the absence of her designing what she really wanted.

So we got intentional and proactive about a redesign.

After dissecting the needs underlying the nightly wine drinking, we designed an initial prototype of what she wanted to do instead. Knowing that she did not want to be impaired during the day so only would drink at night, she chose to replace the need for stress reduction with journaling on gratitude. She also put a reminder note on the fridge, which is the location in the sequence that would trigger the first drink, stating "you have choice" with a heart on it.

A few months later, she shared with me her progress. She had returned to an occasional glass of wine but keeps herself in balance with the journaling and evening yoga. She described, "The most helpful part of the design was to focus on taking control. That was the missing piece. Once I had that confidence built up, I could play with it. I know that I am not bad if I do have a drink, but that I also have the power to exercise my conscious choice and feel empowered." Just as we covered in chapter 8 that our future self can build trust with the past self by following up on the intended behavior design, my friend had restored the relationship between her two temporal selves.

Every behavior exists for a reason, without exception. Ultimately, we are behaviorally efficient beings— nothing remains in our behavior unless it is working for us on some level to help us defend against and survive our situation. My mentor Jon Young teaches about rituals and traditions passed down by indigenous peoples, reminding us that "these are cultures that were about subsistence and survival. Therefore, any tribal ritual or behavior that persists under such harsh conditions serves a very pragmatic use." Likewise, we live through a constant barrage of social, economic, political, and environmental challenges. We are raised in dysfunctional families, high-pressure educational institutions, fast-moving social norms, demanding personal lives, and cutthroat workplaces. You better believe our unconscious fast brains have developed layers and layers of go-to "plays" that help us cope with and endure all of it.

We're attached to this web of conditioned behavior. It's part of us; it gets embedded in our sense of *Me*. This interconnected web of behaviors and needs is what makes it so hard to change behavior. We give up a behavior that may be fulfilling a vital but hidden need. Like pulling on a loose thread of a sweater, once we remove the surface behavior, we find that it is connected to a whole sequence of this web—sometimes leaving us cold and naked. Sometimes it's easier to just leave the sweater on. This is the core of relapse. As we learned before, behavior change creates a sensation of *Not Me*, causing us to feel like the wrong thumb is on top. It's visceral. But even deeper than the brain sending this awkward signal of *Not Me*, we have disrupted a sense of safety. We have unearthed an attachment that drives that specific behavior to repeat itself. We yell at our children whenever we need to control them. We watch a video when we are lonely. We drink when we need to let off steam. It is a pattern I lovingly call the Law of Conservation of Behavior.

LAW OF CONSERVATION OF BEHAVIOR

Let's review. The fast brain is a set of shortcuts that our brain creates to manage the overwhelming volume of sensory stimuli coming at us every second and the deci-sions we need to make as a result. Our responses get pruned down to those that appear to be working for us—and this becomes our playbook of habitual responses. Unconsciously, our go-to plays are run over and over until they show signs of a consequence that becomes progressively more painful. At some tipping point, the pain hits a level we can no longer tolerate—we can't fit into our jeans, our relationship is failing, our finances are draining, and so on. Then and only then are we attentive to the need to change. Then and only then do we iter-ate and tinker. But first, we grieve. We grieve the loss of our favorite thing, our creature comfort, our escape, our addiction. And we pass through the stages of grief.

One of my mentors, Dr. Hans Steiner, a child and adolescent psychiatrist, has taught me that denial, the first stage of grief, is the most primitive form of self-defense. In this stage, we may act childish—like sneaking food—try-ing to test the boundaries, like *do I really have to stop this?*

When I started to accumulate back fat, driven off of a pretty nasty addiction to a sugary (as in 53 grams of sugar!) hot chai drink I enjoyed every morning, it took me at least six months to get over my denial and admit that my chai was the main driver of this unwanted change. In our second stage of grief, we get angry. In my case, I took my anger out on myself—with a lot of private self-flogging and self-loathing speech inside of my head for continuing to drink my chai. Then bargaining sets in. With my back fat, I joined a gym and I worked out harder so that I could keep the chai. When that didn't work, I tried to drink the smaller size, harm reduction-style, thinking that would help me.

Finally, we accept that we are attached, that we have a problem and we need to do something about it. For my chai addiction, I realized that drinking even the tiniest cup was not going to solve my back fat problem, that I was a middle-aged woman and it was just too easy now to gain body fat. As I mentioned in the first chapter, I took to designing—and iterating on my design. I reorganized my fridge, as I mentioned. I started a high-intensity boot camp so I would push past the fact that I could no longer make myself workout hard enough when I was alone—because it hurt! The social norms of the class helped me push myself. But also everyone was so exhausted doing their own station that they did not have the energy to judge and compare others. Finally, I engineered a sugar-free, homemade chai that I have made every day using teabags, unsweetened almond milk, and natural stevia sweetener. (I'm happy to send you my recipe if you send an e-mail request!)

But let's unpack this. Why did these designs work? Why did I need all of them? Here is my analysis.

My hot sugary chai addiction was a behavior that was fulfilling a number of needs. This is why just working out more or reducing the quantity did not work—I had not checked off all the boxes of behavior conservation with those early prototypes. Here is a list of all the functional needs I was meeting with the chai:

1. I worked from home by myself during East Coast hours. I am not a morning person. Going out to get my chai fix got me out of the house, helped me face the cold morning, warmed me up, and created a soothing pleasure. It also gave me a little kick of caffeine to help me wake up and match the frenetic energy of my East Coast colleagues. (I absolutely love East Coasters, but they do kill themselves with stress, self-flogging, and overstimulation.)
2. I got to go to the "cool kids" coffee shop with all the other affluent people who could pay $5 for their drink. It signaled my financial success and security. I also enjoyed interacting with people in my local

community and even the brief friendly exchange with the baristas gave me a sense of connection.

3. I have always had a sweet tooth. I also loved milk as a kid—I don't know, maybe because I was not breast fed? (Deeper therapy needed for that, I guess.) The sensory heuristics of warm, sweet milk is something that soothes me and makes me feel like I can get through the day. It gives me a little self-nurturing "me time" ritual at the start of my day so I can muster the courage to finish the stuff that is staring me down from the day before.

4. Oh, and then there was that morning bowel movement—made perfectly clockwork by the hot chai. Yes, I actually just referenced my bowel movement—because it was honestly part of the matrix of needs that were sitting under my hot chai behavior. (And because medical school made me more comfortable with discussing bodily functions than the average person.)

One cup of chai. A giant web of comfort and satisfaction.

My design approach? Design for every single one of the needs related to the chai. Whack-a-mole-style—I would fix one chai-dependent need and another would pop-up. I would relapse often in the beginning. But as the aggregate of my designs would clot the bleeding of my needs going unmet, I relapsed less often. At the time of this writing, I am at a pace of about one relapse every two months and counting down.

Piggybacking on concepts from physics, I like to call this the Law of Conservation of Behavior (and I am capitalizing it to make it more scientifically official looking, *smile). It emulates the law of conservation of energy in physics, which states that energy cannot be created or destroyed during a chemical reaction. Energy simply changes its form. The Law of Conservation of Behavior similarly states that behaviors are never created or destroyed—they change form or find a substitute. Think of it as each behavior in your whole repertoire of behaviors holding a certain amount of energy—or fulfilling a specific aspect of your needs. If you get rid of one behavior, then that energy has to go somewhere. The energy of unmet needs fuels another behavior to replace the first. This is like alcoholics who smoke cigarettes as a conservation of their addiction behavior. Or they become addicted to sex or something else. In this way, the old behavior is not destroyed; it just changes form. Any unmet need will quickly seek gratification through another channel when its original behavioral outlet gets taken away.

Given that we cannot alter one behavior without disrupting the needs it serves, we must consider each behavior as part of a complex ecosystem that possesses a specific equilibrium. Some people live with a high degree of stress and drama in their lives. As a result, their bodies defend against this relentless drama by consuming sugar and fat-rich foods and storing tremendous belly fat. This is their ecosystem's equilibrium, balancing the stress with the belly fat. Of course, it is not healthy in the long term—most of our coping behaviors are not calibrated for long-term benefits. Nevertheless, the equilibrium and conserved behavior must be calculated into our design. For example, if we just address the side effects of binge eating and do not deal with the root cause of the behavior, stress, or the need for relief and escape that it serves, we violate the Law of Conservation of Behavior. Our design will "leak" with relapse, much like my early attempts to stop drinking hot sugary chai. If we do not address the need for stress reduction, it will show up elsewhere in a slightly disguised form, like having a glass of wine every night, then two, then three.

A simple everyday example is to consider a person with a cluttered desk who decides they need to get organized because it is an eyesore. Maybe they go out and buy some snazzy organizing shelves and bins, all kinds of pricey new stuff to wrangle the clutter and get it out of sight. As they place the last pen in its holder, they smile upon their hard work with pride and satisfaction.

But the design is flawed. As vexing as the clutter may have been, there was an order to the madness. Now that the desk is clean and everything is filed away, the person may forget things, or, worse, miss deadlines. The things on the desk had served as behavior triggers for when certain work was due. The clutter had provided a system that had evolved to be functional and supportive of their work in some ways. They had known where everything was ("halfway down in that stack of papers on the left"), even though to everyone else it looked like a squirrel's nest. Disrupting the clutter disrupted the underlying system of needs it met. The placement (or misplacement) of each item on the desk served a function, and any new design must conserve each behavior that was supported by the old version.

Assuming that everything we are habitually doing has a reason for being (or maybe multiple reasons), we can trace back the cause of a behavior to its source. As we examined in chapter 6, the environment can be a strong source of triggers for existing behaviors. Now, in this chapter, we're layering on the idea that we are attached to either the status quo or a desire for something better. This causes us to self-trigger even without any outside peer pressure or environmental triggers— like when we sabotage our progress by self-triggering ourselves to do the old behavior. For example, we may have let go of partying hard in college, but when we go back for homecoming we are attached to being the life of the party again—and we self-trigger ourselves into getting drunk.

Going back to the earlier example of my friend enjoying her wine in the evenings, the wine drinking was a conserved behavior from her attachment to blowing off steam, which she used to do in healthier ways, when her life was less stressed and she had time to go out to dinner with friends. In our design conversation, she and I anticipated that removing the drinking behavior cold turkey would expose a need to blow off steam and be a rebel. Our design substituted for these behaviors and checked both of those boxes of need. She could blow off steam with her journaling and yoga while maintaining her ability to rebel less often with a less frequent glass of wine after she restored trust with her future self.

Our culture is good at delivering macho messages about stopping suddenly and going cold turkey, but as we discussed, this risks overstretching the rubber band to snap back hard. Rarely do we have an epiphany so clear and strong that we can stop doing a consequential behavior suddenly and never return. Sometimes this does happen. For example, in the case of PTSD, someone is so negatively affected by an event that afterward they avoid all experiences associated with the traumatic event. Their neurochemistry delivered a wallop of cortisol, epinephrine, norepinephrine, and endorphins so powerful that the neurons immediately melted into a fight or flight network that sets up like cement in the brain. This provides a fast track into the fast brain such that whenever the trauma is retriggered, this network fires first and dominates.

Physicians pray for epiphanies to happen to patients. We even are trained to say things like, "If you don't stop, this will kill you" to try to evoke such a fear in patients that they stop. We are not taught about conserved behavior and how to design for it.

The Law of Conservation of Behavior implies that the way that we behave provides some level of comfort, ease, relief, or protection. Satisfaction comes from feeling the ground under our feet. All of those self-soothing and self-protective feelings feed our sense of *Me* and help us feel normal. When we change our behavior, we disrupt the equilibrium. To change the way we do things uncovers deep-seated insecurities and a feeling of *Not Me*. To venture into the territory of *Not Me* is an uncomfortable place to be, so it is no wonder at all that we are attached to the ways things currently are. We often don't change because of our underlying attachments of one kind or another.

LAW OF IMPERMANENCE

One of life's truths is that everything is changing constantly. This is a primary precept of Buddhism as well as a more recently established scientific truth. Working on letting go of attachments is a process—indeed, it is a life-long journey if we think of letting go of all attachments. This is the basis of many psychological philosophies and practices. Letting go takes a lot of diligent work! We get attached to how things are, which sets us up for suffering. We want things to stay the same, but they don't. They just don't. They cannot. Everything in the universe is in constant flux. Everything is subject to change. From a quantum mechanics perspective, all particles that make up everything are not discrete and unchanging matter but are continually in motion and connected. There we go! The basis of life is change, flow, and impermanence. We must change or be changed.

As a mother reinventing how I wanted to raise my daughters to develop their own life philosophy and spirituality, I decided I would teach them only two concepts that I felt I *knew* were truth: impermanence and gratitude. Whenever they would cry about something, like their ice cream cone falling to the ground, and needed to be consoled, I would first tenderly express my condolences for their loss, and then if they couldn't let go, I would ask, "Sweethearts, what is the number one rule of life?" "Everything changes," they would sigh through their disappointment. As they grew up, the ice cream turned into their parents' divorce, their best friend moving away, getting their first bad grade, and breaking up with their crush. In every cycle of attachment and its loss, they developed a comfort level with change—it got easier and they became more resilient.

It sounds harsh to encourage a child to let go of their fallen ice cream. Our society teaches that loss is avoidable, that we are justified to hold on to our grief, that we are victims of change. It encourages us to cling to what we have, pursue compensation for our losses or even retaliate for any change imposed upon us unexpectedly. But I think this way of fighting the law of impermanence weakens us because it goes against the inevitable.

Instead, I believe the answer lies in the elegance of designing. A designer exists in a state of creative experimentation and discovery. A designer accepts the limits of what is but aspires to improve it—intelligently, not foolishly.

Therefore, the practice of letting go of attachments is a vital tool of a designer. After all, how can you iterate if you are so attached to fixed notions that the solution is X, and you are sure it is X, so you waste all of your energy forcing your X design upon your future self, or upon others, insisting you are correct? Like Don Quixote, you repeatedly charge at your own personal windmill like a crazy person. That is not iteration. Iteration means you listen, you have compassion, you change your angle, make an adjustment, and then try again. Honoring the Law of Conservation of Behaviors means that you look upon your attachments with compassion and try your best to replace your behaviors with healthier alternatives that still "check the box" for meeting your underlying needs.

Aging is the perfect teacher of impermanence. It naturally brings a constant lifelong stream of lessons in letting go. I have been an active, albeit flawed, practitioner of using aging to relax my attachments. Even though I suffer a lot of attachment to being pretty, young, and healthy from being praised throughout my young life for that self-image, I believe practicing letting go of these attachments is one of the most important ways to use design toward being happier.

My struggle with aging as a woman in this society forced me to recognize the attachments that come along with the "pretty, young, healthy" self-image of *Me*. A key example of this was my habit of getting male attention in public. It is easy for a young woman to feed off of the thrill of turning heads, even getting addicted to it for her self-worth, and I was no different. When I turned 30 and after having two kids, I realized that this was a path of great suffering for me because I was assuming the role of an object for men to ogle. I was married at the time and this had nothing to do with wanting to cheat; it was just about having my self-image reflected back to me, so I felt like *Me*. And I also had the foresight that if I did not stop this ego feeding on my own, Father Time would inevitably do it for me—because physical beauty as defined by this society is ephemeral. I knew that I had better do something about it lest I end up a desperate, empty, older version of myself—searching for compliments and the increasingly infrequent head turn.

I started to let go of my attachment by not playing this game with the world anymore. I started to avert my eyes when any guy showed me attention. I repeatedly ignored men's attraction to me so that I could taper off of the drug that I had become addicted to. I did things like "fast" for a whole month without makeup or hair products—even going to important business meetings looking like I had just rolled out of bed! For a girl who was raised in Oklahoma, where it seemed you could get arrested for going to the mailbox in anything less than full hair and makeup, this was a big deal. My efforts were loosening the chains of my own vain attachments.

Today, I am extremely grateful to my past self for designing these ways to detach because I am freer now than I otherwise would be. Freer—but not free! As a designer of my own behavior, I fight every day to practice self-love and compassion so that I can manage these attachments and continue to cut the cord they have on my life.

Our attachments get in the way of our embracing the law of impermanence. We find it hard to embrace change. This is such a universal theme that stories of resisting change have been told throughout history. One example from the Bible is the parable of Jesus and the rich man, a story that is often misinterpreted. Inspired by his teachings, a rich man comes to Jesus and says, "Master, I want to serve you." Jesus says, "Go home, sell all of your riches and give to the poor, then come follow me." The rich man becomes sad and goes away, prompting Jesus' comment to the crowd, "How hard it is for a rich man to enter the kingdom of heaven! It is easier for a camel to pass through the eye of a needle!" (Paraphrased from Mt 19:16–30) And many people think that this condemns wealth as bad because it separates you from Spirit. But viewing it through the eyes of a behavior designer, it is really a story about attachments that prevent you from fulfilling your heartfelt desire to be a better person. The rich man was sad because he was attached—clearly he was not ready for that much change.

And this is why we stay. We stay in our miserable relationship because we are afraid of what we will lose if we end it. We hesitate from pursuing our dream career because we are afraid of bankruptcy or abandonment by loved ones. We stop short of spiritual awakening because we are afraid someone will confront us and ask us to sell everything we have and follow the spiritual path—and it scares us into justifying our attachments.

LETTING GO

It can help to think of giving up attachments or surrendering in a gradual fashion—to start moving in the direction of letting the attachments go but not letting go all at once. It doesn't have to be all at once like Jesus and the rich man. In fact, you will more likely succeed if you let go little by little, so your sense of *Me* adjusts to the change over time.

One method of letting go is to substitute the thing to which you are attached with something similar. This aligns with the Law of Conservation of Behavior in that you replace the unhealthy behavior with something that will check off all the boxes for your needs and be a satisfying replacement for your attachments. My story of replacing the expensive, sugary chai with my own homemade concoction is an example of this. I needed a substitute for my sweet tooth—which appears to be here to stay! Other examples of healthy food substitutions include using whipped cauliflower instead of mashed potatoes, using brown instead of white rice, and using stevia instead of sugar and artificial sweeteners. Examples of activity substitutions include mounting television screens on exercise equipment to replace couch potato TV watching; practicing tai chi, which is gentle on older joints but still trains balance; and swimming, which burns fat for lean mass and is easy on weight-bearing joints.

One Colorado Springs woman I interviewed, Catherine, has designed her health using an elaborate system to test new vitamins and supplements in exchange for her old reliable ones. She is optimizing her health through substituting new and better versions of her previous nutrient regimen. And it is working for her—she claims that she overcame both depression and debilitating arthritis using this method. The point is that she is already a designer, even if she does not call it that. Fully in charge of her health and experience, she is getting results through iterating.

Another teaching I have found useful is the practice of giving away. In the Native American part of my ancestry, we have always had a custom of "giveaways." This practice is slightly different across a number of individual tribes, but the basic gist is to hold a celebration in which you as the host give away items of high worth or meaning to you. This is done to celebrate anything positive, like a graduation or even surviving through a hard time. It expresses our appreciation to the Spirit for all of the gifts that have been learned or experienced— no matter if they are were pleasant or unpleasant. It acknowledges and trusts the process of life and the confidence needed to give things away, knowing that we do not need to hang on to them to be OK. It is a way of living and practicing gratitude, which is part of keeping the mind light and happy.

The wisdom of this ancient practice is now supported by brain science. It aligns with three of the constituents of well-being taught by famous neuroscientist Dr. Richard Davidson:

1. Ability to rapidly recover from adversity
2. Ability to have a background glow of positive emotion
3. Generosity, which Davidson comments is the most effective way to activate circuits of positive emotion in the brain.[56]

For Native Americans, this practice even extends to giving away things that another person admires—which I have done on occasion, and it is one of the most revealing ways to see what I have been clinging to.

There are many existing practices that people use to design for letting go of attachments. Fasting practices, like Ramadan, Lent, Yom Kippur, and others, help us release our grip on attachments to food or water, allowing us to focus on deeper contemplation. I, personally, have fasted from weird attachments like french fries and even gossip, in order to release them.

Don't get me wrong, this is not about being some ascetic. I am not a purist. There is nothing wrong with wealth, beautiful things, and pleasurable experiences. The trick is to be honest about where you go all Gollum from the Lord of the Rings about these beautiful things— "my preeeeeeecious!" Attachments are hard to see when and where they start to stick to us, until impermanence shows us where we were leaning on our attachment to something a little too much. Can you lose your appearance and still be OK? What about your reputation? Money? Career? Family? Practicing letting go of attachments does not make you apathetic; it makes you honest and present, cherishing what is here and resting in the wisdom that this too shall pass. Adopting this point of view not only makes you a better designer, it ensures your solidity as a person.

This is my wish for you—to be fully in your power as the designer of your life and to be fully flexible and receptive when life designs you back.

Letting Go Practices

CUTTING THE CORDS

Here is one way to ease your way into a practice of letting go. I learned this from my meditation teacher Sylvia, who at the age of 19 gave up being a college student at a top university to devote her life to awakening her mind and helping others do the same for themselves (talk about giving up attachments!).

Find a place where you can close your eyes and practice visualization without disruption so that you can go deep. Read each instruction, follow it with your eyes closed, then open your eyes and read the next instruction.

1. Begin by thinking of something, someone, or some experience you are attached to. Reflect until you identify an attachment that you want to work on right now. Picture how that attachment is like an umbilical cord, holding you back from being free.

How does it hold you back from your own full expression, from learning or doing new things, from growing? Consider this with your eyes closed for a few minutes. Write down any insights, and read on.

_____

_____

_____

_____

_____

2. Now that you see the attachment and its cord on your life, picture a pair of scissors in your hand and snip the cord off. When you are done, try to end with a deep breath and exhale with a gentle smile on your face. Take as long as you need and repeat as often as you want.

GENEROSITY PRACTICE

The opposite of attachment is generosity. I do not advocate frivolous generosity because that is just as thoughtless as frivolous spending, but here is an advanced practice that I have found to be extremely freeing for me when letting go of attachments using design thinking.

> Make a list of everything that you are attached to. This includes people, things, personal talents, money, and even secrets that you may be harboring. Ask yourself: "What am I ready to release that would stretch or hurt just a little?" This has to be thoughtful so as to not trigger a bad reaction. A little sting is OK when you let it go. But if letting go is something you are going to later seriously regret, hold a grudge over, feel guilty for, or resent, then you are not ready for that one yet. Finally, ask yourself this: "How am I to release this?" The answer could point to giving away something to a particular person, forgiving someone (including yourself), donating money, or replacing it with something better for you.

Notes

Afterword

We all want to live well. We all want to fully express our gifts, experience creative freedom, be appreciated for what we contribute, or maybe even leave a legacy. This is the essence of being human, of how we draw on the meaning of life.

In this book, we have covered a kaleidoscope of design concepts, each a truth about how our brains and behaviors intersect. We have learned that we must be the designer of our life and experience—to iterate our way to success in all domains of our health, relationships, and well-being. We have learned to understand the importance of compassion practice—and to never cease the flow of compassion as we design. We have explored the asynchrony of our fast and slow brains as well as ways to align the two. We have explored the operating system of our self-image as well as our emotions, motivations, and decisions. Finally, we have considered the roles of self-tracking, relapse, and attachment in the behavior change process.

I realize that each chapter is somewhat of a mini-book. That was intentional. I wanted you to be able to pick this book up any time, even after a long break from it, and read something that inspires you to design. As such, I would encourage you to jump around, come back, or even open it up at random and see what you find.

You drive it. You are in charge. There are no rules. There is no right way or wrong way to read this book, there is only experimentation, curiosity, and insight.

Take what you like and leave the rest—maybe for another day, or not.

May you live well. May you design well. May you live a truly well, designed, life!

Endnotes

1   How Sara Blakely got Spanx started. [VIDEO]
     Inc.com, accessed August 5, 2015, http://www.
     inc.com/sara-blakely/how-sara-blakley-started-
     spanx.html; Sara Blakely, Spanx, *Making her-story*,
     accessed August 5, 2015, http://www.spanx.
     com/-cms-making-her-story

2   El-Erian, M. (2013). Spanx billionaire founder
     redefines failure and inspires others. *The Huffington
     Post*, August 25, 2013, accessed August 5, 2015,
     http://www.huffingtonpost.com/mohamed-a-
     elerian/spanx-billionaire-founder_b_3814723.html

3   Walker, R. (2014). A golden age of design.
     T Magazine, September 22, 2014, accessed
     August 5, 2015, http://tmagazine.blogs.nytimes.
     com/2014/09/22/design-golden-age/?_r=0

4   Edmonds, M. (2015). Top 10 Inventions
     by African-Americans. *How Stuff
     Works*, accessed August 5, 2015, http://
     science.howstuffworks.com/innovation/

inventions/10-inventions-by-african-americans.
htm#page=6

5   Jewell, H. (2014). 18 Inventions by women
    that changed the world. *BuzzFeed*, August
    11, 2014, accessed August 5, 2015,
    http://www.buzzfeed.com/hannahjewell/
    inventions-by-women-that-changed-the-world

6   http://www.npr.org/2011/11/27/142664182/
    most-beautiful-woman-by-day-inventor-by-night

7   Markowsky, G. (2015). Information theory:
    Mathematics. *Encyclopedia Britannica*,
    Accessed August 5, 2015, http://www.
    britannica.com/EBchecked/topic/287907/
    information-theory/214958/Physiology

8   Bechara, A, Damasio, H., Tranel, D & Damasio,
    AR. (1997). Deciding advantageously before
    knowing the advantageous strategy. *Science,*
    275(5304). 1293–1295.

9   Davidson, RJ & Lutz, A. (2008). Buddha's brain:

Neuroplasticity and meditation, *IEEE Signal Processing Magazine*, 25(1), 171-174.

10   Klimecki, OM, Leiberg, S, Ricard, M & Singer, T. (2014). Differential pattern of functional brain plasticity after compassion and empathy training. *Social Cognitive and Affective Neuroscience*, 9(6), 873-879.

11   Kahneman, D. (2013). *Thinking, fast and slow.* New York: Farrar, Straus and Giroux.

12   Wyer Jr., RS. (1997). *The Automaticity of everyday life.* Hillsdale, NJ: Lawrence Erlbaum Associates.

13   Wimmer, GE & Shohamy, D. (2012). Preference by association: How memory mechanisms in the hippocampus bias decisions. *Science, 338*(6104), 270-273.

14   Doll, BB, Hutchison, KE & Frank, MJ. (2011). Dopaminergic genes predict individual differences in susceptibility to confirmation bias. *Journal of Neuroscience, 31*(16), 6188-6198.

15   Banaji, MR & Greenwald, AG. (2013). *Blind spot: Hidden biases of good people.* New York: Delacorte Press.

16   Williams, LE & Bargh, JA. (2008). Experiencing physical warmth promotes interpersonal warmth. *Science 322*(5901), 606-607.

17   McGonigal, K. (2011). *The willpower instinct: How self-control works, why it matters, and what you can do to get more of it.* New York: Avery.

18   Medford, N & Critchley, HD. (2010). Conjoint activity of anterior insular and anterior cingulate cortex: Awareness and response. *Brain Structure and Function, 214*(5–6), 535–549.

19   Northoff, G, Heinzel, A, De Greck, M, Bermpohl, F, Dobrowolny, H & Panksepp, J. (2006). Self-referential processing in our brain: A meta-analysis of imaging studies on the self. *NeuroImage, 31*(1), 440-457.

20   Molinsky, A. (2007). Cross-cultural code-
      switching: The psychological challenges of
      adapting behavior in foreign cultural interactions.
      Academy of Management Review, 32(2), 622-640.

21   Prengaman, K. (2013). Infant immune systems
      set on low to encourage microbiome growth. *Ars
      Technica*, November 10, 2013, accessed August
      7, 2015, http://arstechnica.com/science/2013/11/
      infant-immune-systems-set-on-low-to-encourage-
      microbiome-growth

22   Kazimieras Malys, M, Campbell, L & Malys, N.
      (2015). Symbiotic and antibiotic interactions
      between gut commensal microbiota and host
      immune system. *Medicina (Kaunas), 51*(2), 69-75.

23   Tavris, C & Aronson, E. (2007). *Mistakes were
      made (but not by me): Why we justify foolish beliefs,
      bad decisions, and hurtful acts.* Orlando, FL:
      Harcourt.

24   Ritchie, TD, Sedikides, C & Skowronski, JJ.
      (2015). Emotions experienced at event recall

and the self: Implications for the regulation of self-esteem, self-continuity and meaningfulness. *Memory*, 1-15. doi:10.1080/09658211.2015.1031 678.

25   Christensen, TC, Wood, JV & Barrett, LF. (2003). Remembering everyday experience through the prism of self-esteem. *Personality and Social Psychology Bulletin,* 29(1), 51-62.

26   Sacco, T & Sacchetti, B. (2010). Role of secondary sensory cortices in emotional memory storage and retrieval in rats. *Science,* 329(5992), 649–656.

27   Larsson, M, Willander, J, Karlsson, K & Arshamian, A. (2014). Olfactory LOVER: Behavioral and neural correlates of autobiographical odor memory. *Frontiers in Psychology,* 5, 312.

28   The science of emotions: Jaak Panksepp at TEDxRainier. YouTube, November 9, 2013, accessed August 8, 2015, www.youtube.com/watch?v=65e2qScV_K8

29   Panksepp, J. (2010). Affective neuroscience of the emotional brainmind: Evolutionary perspectives and implications for understanding depression. *Dialogues in Clinical Neuroscience, 12*(4), 533-545.

30   Teo, K. et al. (2013). Prevalence of a healthy lifestyle among individuals with cardiovascular disease in high-, middle- and low-income countries: The Prospective Urban Rural Epidemiology (PURE) study. *Journal of the American Medical Association, 309*(15), 1613-1621.

31   Piff, PK, Dietze, P, Feinberg, M, Stancato, DM & Keltner, D. (2015). Awe, the small self, and prosocial behavior. *Journal of Personality and Social Psychology, 108*(6), 883-899.

32   Determinants of Health. HealthyPeople.gov, accessed August 8, 2015, www.healthypeople.gov/2020/about/foundation-health-measures/Determinants-of-Health.

33   Modified to be gender neutral from the original quote "what a man can be, he must be."

34   Lally, P, Van Jaarsveld, CHM, Potts, HWW &
     Wardle, J. (2010). How are habits formed:
     Modelling habit formation in the real world.
     European Journal of Social Psychology, 40(6),
     998-1009.

35   Hebb, DO. (1949). *The organization of behavior: A
     neuropsychological theory.* New York, NY: Wiley &
     Sons.

36   Mayford, M, Siegelbaum, SA & Kandel, ER.
     (2012). Synapses and memory storage. *Cold Spring
     Harbor Perspectives in Biology, 4*(6), 1-22.

37   Besnard, A, Caboche, J & Laroche, S. (2012).
     Reconsolidation of memory: A decade of debate.
     Progress in Neurobiology, 99(1), 61-80.

38   Song, S. (2009). Consciousness and the
     consolidation of motor learning. *Behavioural Brain
     Research, 196*(2), 180-186.

39   Alexander-Bloch, A, Giedd, JN & Bullmore, E.
     (2013). Imaging structural co-variance between

human brain regions. *Nature Reviews Neuroscience,*
14(5), 322-336.

40 Lally, P, Van Jaarsveld, CHM, Potts, HWW &
Wardle, J. (2010). How are habits formed:
Modelling habit formation in the real world.
European Journal of Social Psychology, 40(6),
998-1009.

41 Norcross, JC, Krebs, PM & Prochaska, JO. (2011).
Stages of change. *Journal of Clinical Psychology,*
67(2), 143-154.

42 Lally, P, Wardle, J & Gardner, B. (2011).
Experiences of habit formation: A qualitative study.
Psychology, Health & Medicine, 16(4), 484-489.

43 Lam, CSP & Vasan, RS. (2010). Heart failure risk:
Lessons from the family. *Congestive Heart Failure,*
16(4), 139-140.

44 Christakis, NA & Fowler, JH. (2007). The spread
of obesity in a large social network over 32 years.
New England Journal of Medicine, 357(4), 370-379.

45   Price, TJ & Inyang, KE. (2015). Commonalities between pain and memory mechanisms and their meaning for understanding chronic pain. *Progress in Molecular Biology and Translation Science, 131,* 409-434.

46   Soon, CS, He, AH, Bode, S & Haynes, JD. (2013). Predicting free choices for abstract intentions.   . *Proceedings of the National Academy of Sciences USA, 110*(15), 6217-6222.

47   Romero, R & Polich, J. (1996). P3(00) habituation from auditory and visual stimuli. *Physiology & Behavior, 59*(3), 517-522.

48   Silver, WS, Mitchell, TR & Gist, ME. (1995). Responses to successful and unsuccessful performance: The moderating effect of self-efficacy on the relationship between performance and attributions. *Organizational Behavior and Human Decision Processes, 62*(3) 286-299.

49   Marsden, KE, Ma, WJ, Deci, EL, Ryan, RM & Chiu, PH. (2015). Diminished neural responses

predict enhanced intrinsic motivation and sensitivity to external incentive. *Cognitive, Affective, & Behavioral Neuroscience, 15*(2), 276-286.

50   Webber, ES, Chambers, NE, Kostek, JA, Mankin, DE & Cromwell, HC. (2015). Relative reward effects on operant behavior: Incentive contrast, induction and variety effects. *Behavioural Processes, 116*, 87-99.

51   Drugan, RC, Christianson, JP, Warner, TA & Kent, S. (2013). Resilience in shock and swim stress models of depression. *Frontiers in Behavioral Neuroscience, 7*(14), 1-8.

52   Prochaska, JO & Norcross, JC. (1994). *Changing for good: The revolutionary program that explains the six stages of change and teaches you how to free yourself from bad habits* New York, NY: W. Morrow.

53   Di Pellegrino, G, Fadiga, L, Fogassi, L, Gallese, V & Rizzolatti, G. (1992). Understanding motor events: A neurophysiological story. *Experimental Brain Research, 91*(1), 76-180.

54   Brizendine, L. (2006). *The Female Brain*, New York, NY: Broadway Books.

55   Simon-Thomas, E & Matt Killingsworth, M. (2015). Findings reported at the Facebook Compassion Research Day, Menlo Park, CA.

56   Davidson, RJ & Begley, S. (2012). *The emotional life of your brain: How its unique patterns affect the way you think, feel, and live—and how you can change them*. New York, NY: Hudson Street Press.

References

CHAPTER 1 REFERENCES

Bargh, JA & Chartrand, TL. (1999). The unbearable automaticity of being. *American Psychologist, 54*(7), 462-479.

Baumeister, RF, Bratslavsky, E, Muraven, M & Tice, DM. (1998). Ego depletion: Is the active self a limited resource? *Journal of Personality and Social Psychology, 74*(5), 1252-1265.

Orbell, S & Verplanken, B. (2010). The automatic component of habit in health behavior: Habit as cue-contingent automaticity. *Health Psychology, 29*, 374-383.

Rebar, AL, Loftus, AM, & Hagger, MS. (2015). Cognitive control and the non-conscious regulation of health behavior. *Frontiers in Human Neuroscience, 9*, 122.

Rhodes, RE & Dickau, L. (2012). Experimental evidence for the intention-behaviour relationship in the physical activity domain: A meta-analysis. *Health Psychology, 31*, 724-727.

Rothman, AJ, Sheeran, P & Wood, W. (2009). Reflective and automatic processes in the initiation and maintenance of dietary change. *Annals of Behavioral Medicine, 38,* 4-17.

Sheeran, P, Gollwitzer, PM & Bargh, JA. (2013). Nonconscious processes and health. *Health Psychology, 32*(5), 460-473.

Webb, TL & Sheeran, P. (2006). Does changing behavioral intentions engender behavior change? A meta-analysis of the experimental evidence. *Psychological Bulletin, 132,* 249-268.

CHAPTER 2 REFERENCES

Conoley, CW, Pontrelli, ME, Oromendia, MF, Carmen Bello, BD & Nagata, CM. (2015). Positive empathy: A therapeutic skill inspired by positive psychology. *Journal of Clinical Psychology, 71*(6), 575-583.

The Dalai Lama. (2002). *An open heart: Practicing compassion in everyday life.* Boston, MA: Back Bay Books.

Eres, R, Decety, J, Louis, WR & Molenberghs, P. (2015). Individual differences in local gray matter density are associated with differences in affective and cognitive empathy. *Neuroimage, 117*, 305-310.

Goleman, D. (2005). *Emotional intelligence: Why it can matter more than IQ.* New York, NY: Bantam Books.

Joeng, JR & Turner, SL. (2015). Mediators between self-criticism and depression: Fear of compassion, self-compassion, and importance to others. *Journal of Counseling Psychology, 62*(3), 453-463.

Ledoux, K. (2015). Understanding compassion fatigue. *Journal of Advanced Nursing, 71*(9), 2041-2050.

Neff, K. (2011). *Self-compassion: The proven power of being kind to yourself.* New York, NY: William Morrow.

Sahdra, BK, Ciarrochi, J, Parker, PD, Marshall, S & Heaven, P. (2015). Empathy and nonattachment independently predict peer nominations of prosocial behavior of adolescents. *Frontiers in Psychology, 6*, 263.

Weiszbrod, T. (2015). Health care leader competencies and the relevance of emotional intelligence. *The Health Care Manager, 34*(2), 140-146.

CHAPTER 3 REFERENCES

Craig, AD. (2009). How do you feel—now? The anterior insula and human awareness. *Nature Reviews Neuroscience, 10*, 59-70.

Gilovich, T, Griffin, D & Kahneman, D. (2002). *Heuristics and biases: The psychology of intuitive judgment.* Cambridge, UK: Cambridge University Press.

Glimcher, PW & Fehr, E. (2013). *Neuroeconomics: Decision making and the brain* (2nd ed.). Waltham, MA: Academic Press.

Jeon, HA & Friederici, AD. (2015). Degree of automaticity and the prefrontal cortex. *Trends in Cognitive Science, 19*(5), 244-250.

Kahneman, D. (2012). The human side of decision making: Thinking things through with Daniel Kahneman,

PhD. *Journal of Investment Consulting, 13*(1), 14.

Kahneman, D & Klein, G. (2009). Conditions for intuitive expertise: A failure to disagree. *American Psychologist, 64*(6), 515-526.

Killingsworth, MA & Gilbert, DT. (2010). A wandering mind is an unhappy mind. *Science, 330,* 932.

Millera, J & Schwarz, W. (2014). Brain signals do not demonstrate unconscious decision making: An interpretation based on graded conscious awareness. *Consciousness and Cognition, 24,* 12-21.

CHAPTER 4 REFERENCES

Craig, AD. (2009). How do you feel—now? The anterior insula and human awareness. *Nature Reviews Neuroscience, 10,* 59-70.

Duarte, C, Ferreira, C, Trindade, IA & Pinto-Gouveia, J. (2015). Body image and college women's quality of life: The importance of being self-compassionate. *Journal of Health Psychology, 20*(6), 754-764.

Evrard, HC, Forro, T & Logothetis, NK. (2012). Von economo neurons in the anterior insula of the macaque monkey. *Neuron, 10*(74), 482-489.

Grilli, MD & Verfaellie, M. (2015). Supporting the self-concept with memory: Insight from amnesia. *Social Cognitive and Affective Neuroscience*, doi: 10.1093/scan/nsv056.

Khalid, A & Quiñonez, C. (2015). Straight, white teeth as a social prerogative. *Sociology of Health & Illness, 37*(5), 782-796.

Lazar, SW et al. (2005). Meditation experience is associated with increased cortical thickness. *Neuroreport, 16*(17), 1893-1897.

Liss, M & Erchull, MJ. (2015). Not hating what you see: Self-compassion may protect against negative mental health variables connected to self-objectification in college women. *Body Image, 14,* 5-12.

Medford, N & Critchley, HD. (2010). Conjoint activity of anterior insular and anterior cingulate cortex: Awareness and response. *Brain Structure and Function*, 214(5-6), 535-549.

Tucker, DM, Poulsen, C & Luu, P. (2015). Critical periods for the neurodevelopmental processes of externalizing and internalizing. *Development and Psychopathology*, 27(2), 321-346.

Zunick, PV, Fazio, RH & Vasey, MW. (2015). Directed abstraction: Encouraging broad, personal generalizations following a success experience. *Journal of Personality and Social Psychology*, 109(1), 1-19.

CHAPTER 5 REFERENCES

Crockett, MJ, Braams, BR, Clark, L, Tobler, PN, Robbins, TW & Kalenscher, T. (2013). Restricting temptations: Neural mechanisms of precommitment. *Neuron*, 79(2), 391-401.

Custers, R & Aarts, H. (2005). Positive affect as implicit motivator: On the nonconscious operation of behavioral goals. *Journal of Personality and Social Psychology*, 89(2), 129-142.

Heatherton, TF & Wagner, DD. (2011). Cognitive neuroscience of self-regulation failure. *Trends in Cognitive Science*, *15*(3), 132-139.

Job, V, Walton, GM, Bernecker, K & Dweck, CS. (2015). Implicit theories about willpower predict self-regulation and grades in everyday life. *Journal of Personality and Social Psychology*, *108*(4), 637-647.

Job, V, Walton, GM, Bernecker, K & Dweck, CS. (2013). Beliefs about willpower determine the impact of glucose on self-control. *Proceedings of the National Academy of Sciences USA*, *110*(37), 14837-14842.

Lopez, RB, Hofmann, W, Wagner, DD, Kelley, WM & Heatherton, TF. (2014). Neural predictors of giving in to temptation in daily life. *Psychological Science*, *25*(7), 1337-1344.

Miller, EM, Walton, GM, Dweck, CS, Job, V, Trzesniewski, KH & McClure, SM. (2012). Theories of willpower affect sustained learning. *PLoS One*, *7* (6):e38680.

Ray, RD & Zald, DH. (2011). Anatomical insights into the interaction of emotion and cognition in the prefrontal cortex. *Neuroscience & Biobehavioral Review*, 36(1), 479-501.

Salzman, CD & Fusi, S. (2010). Emotion, cognition, and mental state representation in amygdala and prefrontal cortex. *Annual Review of Neuroscience*, 33, 173-202.

Wagner, DD, Altman, M, Boswell, RG, Kelley, WM & Heatherton, TF. (2013). Self-regulatory depletion enhances neural responses to rewards and impairs top-down control. *Psychological Science*, 24(11), 2262-2271.

CHAPTER 6 REFERENCES

Bavelier, D, Levi, DM, Li, RW, Dan, Y & Hensch, TK. (2010). Removing brakes on adult brain plasticity: From molecular to behavioral interventions. *Journal of Neuroscience*, 30(45), 14964-14971.

Davidson, RJ & McEwen, BS. (2012). Social influences on neuroplasticity: Stress and interventions to promote well-being. *Nature Neuroscience, 15*(5), 689-695.

Faghihi, F & Moustafa, AA. (2015). The dependence of neuronal encoding efficiency on Hebbian plasticity and homeostatic regulation of neurotransmitter release. *Frontiers in Cellular Neuroscience*, 9, 169.

Fernando, S & Yamada, K. (2012). Spike-timing-dependent plasticity and short-term plasticity jointly control the excitation of Hebbian plasticity without weight constraints in neural networks. *Computational Intelligence and Neuroscience*, 968272. doi: 10.1155/2012/968272.

Francis, JJ, O'Connor, D & Curran, J. (2012). Theories of behaviour change synthesised into a set of theoretical groupings: Introducing a thematic series on the theoretical domains framework. *Implementation Science*, 7, 35.

Hölzel, BK. et al. (2010). Stress reduction correlates with structural changes in the amygdala. *Social Cognitive Affective Neuroscience*, 5, 11-17.

Mapelli, L, Pagani, M, Garrido, JA & D'Angelo, E. (2015). Integrated plasticity at inhibitory and excitatory synapses in the cerebellar circuit. *Frontiers in Cellular Neuroscience*, *9*, 169.

Thompson, AK & Wolpaw, JR. (2015). Targeted neuroplasticity for rehabilitation. *Progress in Brain Research*, *218*, 157-172.

CHAPTER 7 REFERENCES

Appelboom, G, Camacho, E, Abraham, ME, Bruce, SS, Dumont, EL, Zacharia, BE, D'Amico, R, Slomian, J, Reginster, JY, Bruyère, O & Connolly, Jr., ES. (2014). Smart wearable body sensors for patient self-assessment and monitoring. *Archives of Public Health*, *72*(1), 28.

Atienza, AA, Oliveira, B, Fogg, BJ & King, AC. (2006). Using electronic diaries to examine physical activity and other health behaviors of adults age 50+. *Journal of Aging and Physical Activity*, *14*(2), 192-202.

Choe, EK, Lee, B & Schraefel, MC. (2015). Revealing visualization insights from quantified-selfers' personal data presentations. *IEEE Computer Graphics and Application*, *35*(4), 28-37.

Havens, J. (2014). *Hacking happiness: Why your personal data counts and how tracking it can change the world.* New York, NY: Tarcher/Penguin.

Kim, J. (2014). Analysis of health consumers' behavior using self-tracker for activity, sleep, and diet. *Telemedicine Journal and E-Health, 20*(6), 552-558.

Kim, J. (2014). A qualitative analysis of user experiences with a self-tracker for activity, sleep, and diet. *Interactive Journal of Medical Research, 3*(1), e8.

MacManus, R. (2014). *Trackers: How technology is helping us monitor and improve our health.* Kindle Edition. Auckland, NZ: David Bateman Ltd.

Quantified Self: Self Knowledge Through Numbers. Accessed August 15, 2015. http://quantifiedself.com.

CHAPTER 8 REFERENCES

Davis, DE, Ho, MY, Griffin, BJ, Bell, C, Hook, JN, Van Tongeren, DR, DeBlaere, C, Worthington, EL & Westbrook, CJ. (2015). Forgiving the self and physical and mental health correlates: A meta-analytic review.

Journal of Counseling Psychology, 62(2), 329-335.

Diedrich, A, Grant, M, Hofmann, SG, Hiller, W & Berking, M. (2014). Self-compassion as an emotion regulation strategy in major depressive disorder. *Behaviour Research and Therapy*, 58, 43-51.

Galante, J, Galante, I, Bekkers, MJ & Gallacher, J. (2014). Effect of kindness-based meditation on health and well-being: A systematic review and meta-analysis. *Journal of Clinical Psychology*, 82(9), 1101-1114.

Hall, CW, Row, KA, Wuensch, KL & Godley, KR. (2013). The role of self-compassion in physical and psychological well-being. *Journal of Psychology*, 147(4), 311-323.

Homan, KJ & Tylka, TL. (2015). Self-compassion moderates body comparison and appearance: Self-worth's inverse relationships with body appreciation. *Body Image*, 15, 1-7.

Olson, K & Kemper, KJ. (2014). Factors associated with well-being and confidence in providing compassionate care. *Journal of Evidence-Based Complementary and Alternative Medicine*, 19(4), 292-296.

Raab, K. (2014). Mindfulness, self-compassion, and empathy among health care professionals: A review of the literature. *Journal of Health Care Chaplaincy*, 20(3), 95-108.

Smeets, E, Neff, K, Alberts, H & Peters, M. (2014). Meeting suffering with kindness: Effects of a brief self-compassion intervention for female college students. *Journal of Clinical Psychology*, 70(9) 794-807.

CHAPTER 9 REFERENCES

Amireaulta, S, Godin, G & Vézina-Imb, L-A. (2013). Determinants of physical activity maintenance: A systematic review and meta-analyses. *Health Psychology Review*, 7(1), 55-91.

Bentley, F, Tollmar, K, Stephenson, P, Levy, L, Jones, B, Robertson, S, Price, E,

Catrambone, R & Wilson, J. (2013). Health mashups: Presenting statistical patterns between wellbeing data and context in natural language to promote behavior change. *ACM Transactions on Computer-Human Interaction (TOCHI)*, 20(5), Article 30.

Brunstein, A, Brunstein, J & Mansar, SL. (2012). Integrating health theories in health and fitness applications for sustained behavior change: Current state of the art. *Creative Education*, 3(08), 1.

Fleiga, L, Pompa, S, Parschaua, L. et al. (2013). From intentions via planning and behavior to physical exercise habits. *Psychology of Sport and Exercise*, 14(5), 632-639.

Gomersall, S, Maher, C, English, C, Rowlands, A & Olds, T. (2015). Time regained: When people stop a physical activity program, how does their time use change? A randomised controlled trial. *PLoS ONE, 10*(5): e0126665.

Hekler, EB, Buman, MP & Nikhil Poothakandiyil, N. et al. (2013). Exploring behavioral markers of long-term physical activity maintenance: A case study of system identification modeling within a behavioral intervention. *Health Education & Behavior, 40*(1), 51S-62S.

Kahlert, D. (2015). Maintenance of physical activity: Do we know what we are talking about? *Preventive Medicine Reports, 2,* 178-180.

Loef, M & Walach, H. (2015). How applicable are results of systematic reviews and meta-analyses of health behaviour maintenance? A critical evaluation. *Public Health, 129*(4), 377-384.

Romaina, AJ, Attalinb, V, Sultanb, A, Boegnerb, C, Gernigona, C & Avignon, A. (2014). Experiential or behavioral processes: Which one is prominent in physical activity? Examining the processes of change 1 year after an intervention of therapeutic education among adults with obesity. *Patient Education and Counseling, 97*(2), 261-268.

Williams, D, Lewis, B, Dunsiger, S. et al. (2008). Comparing psychosocial predictors of physical activity adoption and maintenance. *Annals of Behavior Medicine, 36,* 186-194.

CHAPTER 10 REFERENCES

Atzil, S, Hendler, T & Feldman, R. (2011). Specifying the neurobiological basis of human attachment: Brain, hormones, and behavior in synchronous and intrusive mothers. *Neuropsychopharmacology*, *36*, 2603-2615.

Chah, A. (2005). *Everything arises, everything falls away: Teachings on impermanence and the end of suffering*. Boston, MA: Shambhala Publications.

Chödrön, P. (2000). *When things fall apart: Heart advice for difficult times*. Boston, MA: Shambhala Publications.

Cozolino, L. (2014). *The neuroscience of human relationships: Attachment and the developing social brain* (*2nd ed.*). New York, NY: W.W. Norton & Co., Inc.

Ein-Dor, T. (2015). Attachment dispositions and human defensive behavior. *Personality and Individual Differences*, *81*, 112-116.

Frewen, PA, Evans, EM, Maraj, N, Dozois, DJA & Partridge, K. (2008). Letting go: Mindfulness and negative automatic thinking. *Cognitive Therapy and*

Research, 32(6), 758-774.

Goldberg, EC. (2013). *Saying no and letting go: Jewish wisdom on making room for what matters most.* Woodstock, VT: Jewish Lights Publishing.

Neala, DT, Wooda, W, Labrecquea, JS & Lally, P. (2012). How do habits guide behavior? Perceived and actual triggers of habits in daily life. *Journal of Experimental Social Psychology*, 48(2), 492-498.

Rostera, CA. (2014). The art of letting go: Creating dispossession paths toward an unextended self. *Consumption Markets and Culture*, 17(4), 321-345.

Walser, M, Goschke, T & Fischer, R. (2014). The difficulty of letting go: Moderators of the deactivation of completed intentions. *Psychological Research*, 78(4), 574-583.

About the Author

Dr. Kyra Bobinet obviously wrote this section so you are about to read what she thinks of herself—which is kinda awkward for both of us—so let me just switch to the first person.

So, here's the deal. I live to serve others. It gets me up in the morning. I want to free myself and others from the suffering we wallow in, or actively deny, every day.

In order to be good at it, and figure out what may help others, I spend a lot of time experimenting on my own behavior. For example, how can I get myself to do things that are good for me (or scary for me plus good for me) without getting stuck in fear, a feeling of worth-lessness, or any other flavor of self-defeating emotion? I am obsessed with what causes us to behave and feel the way we do, so I can be more beneficial to you.

And, in collaboration with others, I have enjoyed great success serving the world. I was fortunate to attend UCSF School of Medicine and Harvard School of Public Health. I have built programs and algorithms that change behavior at the million-person scale. I have changed individual lives through intensive mentoring and coach-ing. I have sought out teachers and wise elders for my own transformations. I delight in teaching at Stanford School of Medicine. I have created a design firm, engagedIN, that helps people and organizations change behavior for the better. For this, I have won accolades and awards (including the 2015 Innovator Award from Harvard T. H. Chan School of Public Health as well as past service awards from UCSF, echoing green, and the mayor of San Francisco).

But it hasn't been enough. I've been restless to give others the best possible solutions so they can reach a whole new level within themselves. And with so many great resources and authors out there, I wondered what I had to offer that was worth saying?

Well, here is what I figured out. My specialty is bringing two medicines to you: behavior change and design thinking. Through my love of science, I can decipher really complicated concepts into useful insights to help you build your self-awareness. Likewise, I am, and always have been, a designer. But unlike classic categories like fashion, interior décor, or graphic design, it turns out I am a designer of things like tranquility, transformation, healing, and behavior change. And I am not alone—I believe that every woman and man does this for their own life everyday—and all they need is to recognize and expand this intuition into full-blown life design skills.

This is why I exist. And why I became an author.

PS. I live in Northern California, am Ojibwe/Bohemian by ancestry, and adore my family (my husband Josh and our mixed brood of Shara, Memphis, Ethan, Alecsa), horses, ecodesign, and surfing!

PPS. I invite you to share your thoughts about and experiences with the book at me@drkyrabobinet.com.

PPPS. Get free bonus supplements to this book and/or sign up for design workshops at www.drkyrabobinet.com